THE MASONIC BOOK CLUB

———— VOL. 4 ————

Illustrations of Masonry
William Preston

Westphalia Press
An Imprint of the Policy Studies Organization
Washington, DC

ILLUSTRATIONS OF MASONRY

All Rights Reserved © 2025 by Policy Studies Organization

Westphalia Press
An imprint of Policy Studies Organization
1367 Connecticut Avenue NW
Washington, D.C. 20036
info@ipsonet.org

ISBN: 978-1-63723-643-7

Daniel Gutierrez-Sandoval, Executive Director
PSO and Westphalia Press

Updated material and comments on this edition
can be found at the Westphalia Press website:
www.westphaliapress.org

The Masonic Book Club

The *Masonic Book Club* (MBC) was formed in 1970 by two Illinois Masons, Alphonse Cerza, 33°, and Louis L. Williams, 33°. The MBC primarily reprinted out-of-print Masonic books with scholarly introductions; occasionally they would print additional texts as "bonuses" (though none were marked specifically as such on the title pages); sometimes a reprint would be marked "Masonic Book Club Edition"; often an unnumbered bonus was published jointly with the Illinois Lodge of Research or the Supreme Council, 33°, NMJ, USA.

Most of the MBC volumes indicated on the title page, "Volume [*Number*] of the Publications of the Masonic Book Club," some were misnumbered, and some were unnumbered. Indeed, the numbering of the early volumes was inconsistent. For example, *A Serious and Impartial Enquiry* is "Volume Five" (1974) but *Masonic Membership of the Founding Fathers* is "The Masonic Book Club Edition" (1974). Then, *Masonry Dissected* is "Volume Eight" (1977), *The Trestleboard* is "Volume 8A" (1978), and *Anderson's Constitutions of 1738* is "Volume Nine" (1978). If nothing else, MBC books keep bibliophiles on their toes.

The first volumes had deckle-edged paper and pages of slightly different sizes, though eventually the MBC settled into a 6"×9" trimmed-page format for their books. The books were bound in a dark blue fabric with gold lettering. Listed below are the fifty-nine MBC volumes published 1970–2010 with bonuses. N.B.: A number and letter, e.g. "Volume 8A," is a numbering for this reprint series.

The club originally was limited to 333 members, but the number grew to nearly 2,000, with 1,083 members when it dissolved in 2010. In 2017 MW Barry Weer, 33°, the last president of the MBC, transferred the MBC name and assets to the Supreme Council, 33°, SJ, USA. Under the editorship of Arturo de Hoyos, 33°, G∴C∴, and S. Brent Morris, 33°, G∴C∴, the revived Masonic Book Club has the goal of publishing classic Masonic books while supporting Scottish Rite, SJ, USA philanthropies.

Publications of the Masonic Book Club, 1970–2010

1	1970	*The Regius Poem*	Masonic Book Club
2	1971	*The Constitutions of the Free-Masons*	Benjamin Franklin
3	1972	*Ahiman Rezon*	Laurence Dermott
4	1973	*Illustrations of Masonry*	William Preston
5	1974	*A Serious and Impartial Enquiry into the Cause of the Present Decay of Free-Masonry in the Kingdom of Ireland*	Fifield D'Assigny
5A	1974*	*Masonic Membership of the Founding Fathers*	Ronald E. Heaton

6	1975	*The Signers of the Declaration of Independence*	David C. Whitney
7	1976	*The Signers of the Constitution of the United States*	Masonic Book Club
7A	1976*	*Masonic Symbols in American Decorative Art*	Louis L. Williams & Alphonse Cerza
8	1977	*Samuel Prichard's Masonry Dissected, 1730*	Harry Carr
8A	1978*	*Trestle-Board (A facsimile of the original Trestle Board by the Baltimore Masonic Convention of 1843)*	Dwight L. Smith
9	1978	*Anderson's Constitutions of 1738*	Lewis Edward & W. J. Hughan
10	1979	*Sufferings of John Coustos*	Wallace McLeod
11	1980	*The Revelations of a Square*	George Oliver
11A	1980	*Biblical Characters in Freemasonry*	John H. Van Gorden
11B	1980*	*A Masonic Reader's Guide*	*Guide* Alphonse Cerza & Thomas Warden
12	1981	*Three Distinct Knocks and Jachin and Boaz*	Harry Carr
13	1982	*Masonic Almanacs and Anti-Masonic Almanacs*	Plez A. Transou
13A	1982*	*Stephen A. Douglas: Freemason*	Wayne C. Temple
14	1983	*The Beginnings of Freemasonry in America*	Melvin M. Johnson
14A	1983*	*Bespangled, Painted & Embroidered: Decorated Masonic Aprons in America, 1790–1850*	Scottish Rite Masonic Museum & Library
14B	1983*	*Making a Mason at Sight*	Louis L. Williams
15	1984	*Masonic Concordance of the Holy Bible*	Charles Clyde Hunt
15A	1984*	*By Square and Compasses: The Building of Lincoln's Home and Its Saga*	Wayne C. Temple

16	1985	*The Old Gothic Constitutions*	Wallace McLeod
16A	1985*	*Modern Historical Characters in Freemasonry*	John H. Van Gorden
17	1986	*The Rise and Development of Organised Freemasonry*	Roy A. Wells
17A	1986*	*Ancient and Early Medieval Historical Characters in Freemasonry*	John H. Van Gorden
18	1987	*The Lodge in Friendship Village and Other Stories*	P. W. George
18A	1987*	*Masonic Charities*	John H. Van Gorden & Stewart M. L. Pollard
18B	1987*	*Medieval Historical Characters in Freemasonry*	John H. Van Gorden
18C	1987*	*George Washington in New York*	Allan Boudreau & Alexander Bleimann
19	1988	*Records of the Hole Crafte and Fellowship of Masons*	Edward Conder, Jr.
20	1989	*A Candid Disquisition of the Principles and Practices of the Most Ancient and Honourable Society of Free and Accepted Masons*	Wellins Calcott
20A	1989*	*Freemasonry and Nauvoo, 1839–1846*	Robin L. Carr
21	1990	*Masonic Odes and Poems*	Rob Morris
22	1991	*Lessing's Masonic Dialogues*	Gotthold Lessing
22A	1991*	*ABC of Freemasonry: A Book for Beginners*	Delmar D. Darrah
23	1992	*The Folger Manuscript*	S. Brent Morris
24	1993	*Freemasonry and Christianity: Lectures from Two Ages*	T. De Witt Peake & John J. Murchison
25	1994	*The Constitutions of St. John's Lodge*	Robin L. Carr
25A	1994*	*The Mystic Tie and Men of Letters*	Robin L. Carr
26	1995	*Recollections of a Masonic Veteran*	S. Brent Morris

27	1996	*The Freemason's Monitor or Illustrations of Masonry in Two Parts*	Thomas Smith Webb
28	1997	*The Masonic Ladder or the Nine Steps to Ancient Freemasonry*	John Sherer
28A	1997*	*Freemasonry and Democracy: Its Evolution in North America*	Allen E. Roberts & Wallace McLeod
29	1998	*The Masonic Harp: Collection of Masonic Odes, Hymns, Songs*	George Wingate Chase
30	1999	*Symbolic Teachings of Masonry and Its Message*	Thomas Milton Stewart
31	2000	*Freemasonry Its Meaning and Significance, An Exposition of its Ethics, Religion and Philosophy*	Otto Caspari
32	2001	*K. R. Cama Masonic Jubilee Volume*	Jivanji Jamshedji Modi
33	2002	*Caementaria Hibernica*	W. J. Chetwode Crawley
34	2003	*A Daily Advancement in Masonic Knowledge*	Wallace McLeod & S. Brent Morris
35	2004	*The Craftsman, and Templar's Textbook and, also, Melodies for the Craft*	Cornelius Moore
36	2005	*The Text Book of Freemasonry*	Retired Member of the Craft
37	2006	*Orations of the Illustrious Brother Frederick Dalcho Esq., M.D.*	Frederick Dalcho
38	2007	*Antiquities of Freemasonry Comprising Illustrations of the Five Grand Periods of Masonry from the Creation of the World to the Dedication of King Solomon's Temple*	George Oliver
39	2008	*Diogenes' Lamp or an Examination of our Present-Day Morality and Enlightenment*	Adam Weishaupt
40	2009	*Proofs of Conspiracy Against All the Governments of Europe*	John Robison
41	2010	*The Evolution of Freemasonry*	Delmar Darrah

* *indicates a bonus book*

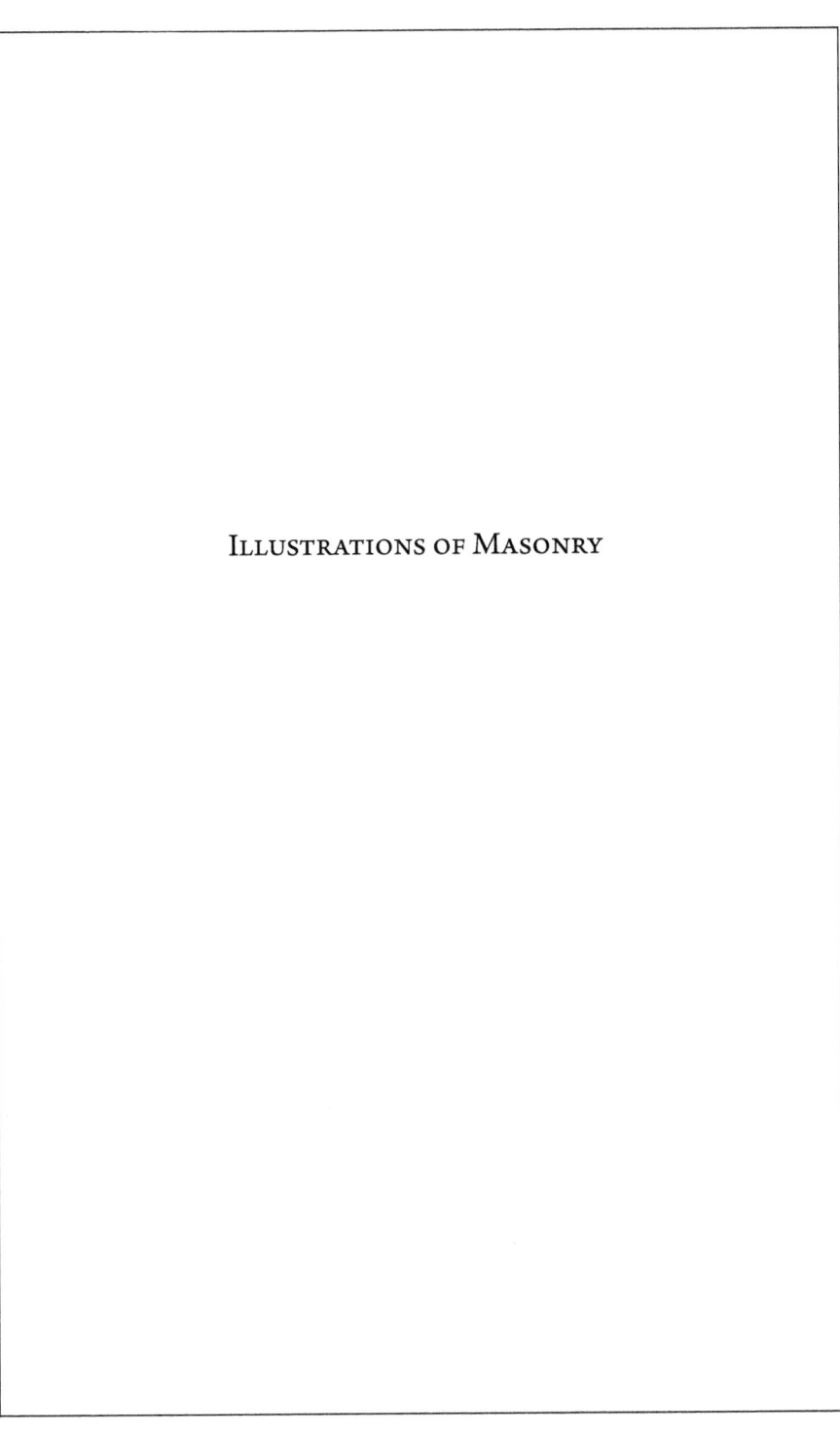

Illustrations of Masonry

ILLUSTRATIONS OF MASONRY

WILLIAM PRESTON

A facsimile reprint of the
Second Edition of
1775

VOLUME FOUR
of the Publications of
THE MASONIC BOOK CLUB

Published by
THE MASONIC BOOK CLUB
A Not-for-Profit Corporation of Illinois
Bloomington, Illinois
1973

Table of Contents

Preface	vii
Foreword—Walter M. Callaway, Jr.	ix
Title Page	1
Dedication	A2
"The Sanction"	A3
Preface	A5
Contents	xviii
"A Vindication of Masonry"	1
Remarks on Masonry	43
"The Principles of Masonry"	149
Collection of Odes, Anthems and Songs	275
Bibliography	301
Colophon	303

Preface

How fortunate are the members of The Masonic Book Club, in that there are so many Masons willing to share their treasures with their Brother Masons. When Brother Walter M. Callaway, Jr., editor of *The Masonic Messenger of Georgia*, offered to lend us the keystone of his collection of Masonic books, a very rare second edition of Preston, for the purpose of preparing the facsimile plates, and in addition offered to write the Preface, you may readily imagine our unbridled enthusiasm, and our joy at being able to present this volume to our members.

So here it is, ranking just behind *Anderson's Constitutions* as probably the second most important Masonic book ever published. Its influence on our ritual structure cannot be overestimated. Brother Callaway speaks of its use in Georgia. Speaking of Illinois ritual, Preston is followed in literally hundreds of phrases.

Preston conceived of Masonry as a great educational force. He collected, refined and polished its language and imagery, and left us a Masonic heritage to last throughout the centuries.

Louis L. Williams
Alphonse Cerza

Foreword

William Preston was one of the most important Freemasons of his day. This appraisal can be made on the basis of the work he did within the Craft in his lifetime, as well as the influence of his book on the development of the Masonic ritual in England and in the United States. It is a pity that his name is virtually unknown today in Masonic circles.

Occasionally his name rates a bare reference in the footnotes of Masonic chronicles, particularly in the monitors and manuals used in the United States. It may well be that his pioneer writings on the Masonic ritual are used more in United States lodges today than they are or have been in England since the Union of 1813. Preston's first edition of *Illustrations of Masonry* in 1772 served to bring ritualistic order out of chaos. It was the first book published containing the lectures, forms and ceremonies of the Lodge. It is well to bear in mind that prior to Preston's day lodges were primarily conviviality clubs for the enjoyment and merriment of the Brethren. Preston looked deeper into Freemasonry and found something far beyond and deeper than mere sociability. His book and lectures were designed to show or "illustrate" that the Craft and its ritual were designed to teach moral lessons and improve the character of its members.

In Preston's time it was customary to have a sponsor when publishing a book and to dedicate the work to some important person. The 1775 edition of *Illustrations of Masonry* was dedicated to Lord Petre, Grand Master of Masons in England from 1772 to 1776. Lord Petre was one of the three Roman Catholics who served as Grand Masters in England. He was a leading Catholic layman in England even while serving five years as Grand Master.

It is said that Lord Petre later left the Craft on account of his church but his interest never waned in Freemasonry and that Masonic Charity always found a generous purse with him.

William Preston was born in 1742 at Edinburgh, Scotland, and died in 1818 at London. His father, also William Preston, was a lawyer and in comfortable financial circumstances. Young Preston received many educational advantages early in life. Following the death of the elder Preston he moved to London in 1760 where he became associated with a leading publishing house as editor and corrector. This work brought

Preston into contact with many of England's most noted literary figures. In 1762 he became a Freemason in London and from then until his death in 1818 he was highly active in the affairs of the Craft. It was as Worshipful Master of the Time Immemorial Lodge of Antiquity that Masonic fame began to come to Brother Preston. A bachelor all his life, he was consumed with two interests in life,—his profession and Freemasonry. At his death in 1818 he willed his entire estate to three Masonic purposes: the General Charity Fund of Grand Lodge; the Royal Freemasons' Charity for Female Children; the remaining one-third to Grand Lodge to establish funds to provide for the annual delivery of lectures.

The annual Prestonian lectures are the only Lectures held under the authority of the United Grand Lodge of England. The Lectures were given for many years and then lapsed for some sixty years. Interest accumulated on the invested funds, some three hundred pounds left by Preston, so in 1924 the Lectures were revived in new form and, except for the war years, 1940 to 1946, have been delivered annually since that time. Originally the Preston bequest required that the Lecturer be some well-informed Freemason to deliver annually a lecture on the First, Second or Third Degree of the Order of Masonry according to the system practiced in the Lodge of Antiquity during Preston's Mastership. Now the Lecturer is free to pick his own Masonic topic subject to certain limitations. To be chosen as the Prestonian Lecturer is one of the highest academic honors which can come to a Freemason.

In 1965 Quatuor Coronati Lodge No. 2076, premier Masonic research lodge, published *The Collected Prestonian Lectures*, 1927-1960, inclusive. This book of valuable Masonic information has 480 pages, was edited by W. Bro. Harry Carr, Secretary of the lodge and a member of the Advisory Board of The Masonic Book Club. Publication was by permission of the Board of General Purposes of the United Grand Lodge of England. Thus, in still another way, William Preston lives with us today.

Prior to the publication of his first, or 1772 edition of *Illustrations*, Preston, from his own personal funds, had employed men to range far and wide searching for old Masonic documents, and visiting lodges to observe the forms and ceremonies being used therein, mostly in the field of ritualism. He collated what had been found, probably added many of his own thoughts and observations, and then worked his material up into an orderly fashion, a systematized form. After much discussion with his friends Preston called for a "Grand Gala" in London in early 1772 and there he delivered an oration on Freemasonry based on his findings and his opinions. At the London lodge for the occasion were many brethren, some of Grand Lodge rank. The affair was so successful and approval was so widespread that the oration was put into book form and the first edition of *Illustrations of Masonry* resulted in 1772.

A word at this point seems in order and this concerns the word "Illustrations." There are no pictures in the book. Today we think of "illustrations" in terms of photographs or drawings and the like. This book was written almost two hundred years ago. The Oxford Dictionary gives the following definitions of "Illustration": 1581: "make clear or evident" and in 1717, "to light up, illuminate," in 1748, "to beautify and adorn." The word is defined sometimes as "to enlighten", and this is what Brother Preston was trying to do.

In the Preface of the 1775 edition (xiii) Preston wrote a message concerning his beliefs in the duties of a Worshipful Master towards his Brethren, a passage which, alone, would have justified Preston's fame, and which, I think, should be transmitted, word for word to every Master-elect of every Masonic lodge.

An eminent American Freemason, Thomas

Smith Webb, in 1797, published a book which he named *Illustrations of Masonry, or Freemasons' Monitor*. Webb, in the preface of his second or 1801 edition, of which I have a copy, states that he copied from Preston "in the first three degrees . . . with some necessary alterations" which he described as more suitable for American work. H. L. Haywood, Masonic scholar of Iowa, (1886-1956) in Masonic Curiosa (Missouri Lodge of Research, 1968) stated Webb was visited by two English brothers who imparted the esoteric work which they had learned from Preston's work in the principal Lodges of Instruction in London. On pages 170-171, of the same volume, Brother Haywood informs us that when the tenth edition of Preston reached America that two printers, one in Portsmouth, N.H., the other in Alexandria, Va., decided, unknown to each other, to print the edition. Haywood said of Preston: "As time passes, the figure of Preston looms larger against the background of Masonic history. Instead of growing less, his shadow increases. The high statue of his fame, and all cynics to the contrary notwithstanding, has never yet been found to have feet of clay. Preston was a much bigger man than his reputation gives him credit for. . . ."

It would be well-nigh impossible for one man to be familiar with the ritualism as practiced in forty-nine grand jurisdictions of the United States. To evaluate the present influence of William Preston's ritualism requires me to resort to the ritualism of the Lodges of my own State of Georgia, and what is found in the *Manual and Code* (1963) of the Grand Lodge of Georgia, F&AM, particularly in the part which contains the Manual—the forms, lectures and ceremonies of an esoteric nature. It is readily apparent that there is a very close similarity between *Illustrations of Masonry* and our own Manual. But the name of Preston is no more than a footnote while we find nearly every ceremony, form, etc., almost verbatim from Preston's work. Georgia's mother Lodge, Solomon's No. 1, Savannah, was warranted by the Grand Lodge of England in 1735, about seven years prior to the birth of William Preston.

One passage in particular is worth noting as an example of semi-verbatim language. On page 62 of *Illustrations of Masonry* is found the charge at initiation: "In the State you are to be a quiet and *peaceable subject*. . . ." (italics mine). When Brother Webb copied Preston he left *peaceable subject* intact. In the same charge of Georgia *Masonic*

Manual and Code we read: "In the State, you are to be a quiet and peace*ful subject* (italics mine). . . ."

Why *peaceable* was changed to *peaceful* we cannot answer. The word "subject" as applied to Americans after 1776 is erroneous. In Great Britain it is still correct. In 1797, when Webb copied Preston for the first time, it would seem that he would have changed "subject" to "citizen." Brother Webb let this slip by him and the error persists to this day in Georgia.

The "work" in the various American States became known as the Webb-Preston Work, something of a misnomer since Brother Webb, in the three degrees, was little more than a copier of Preston. The expression Webb-Preston Work is rarely heard today. To take the time to study and compare Preston's *Illustrations of Masonry* with our Manuals, *Monitors*, etc., is an exercise in Masonic interest and enjoyment. It is my conviction that each such book, based on Preston's work, should have a brief preface acknowledging the source of whatever may have emanated from Preston and found in that book. William Preston, dead these 155 years, deserves more than just an occasional footnote in our documents. For as long as his work lasts, directly or indirectly, his name should be kept fresh.

To omit mention of how I happened to acquire this second edition of Preston, said to be the best of all the many editions of *Illustrations of Masonry*, would be to stop singing before the song was over. Several years of fruitless search had been made for a copy. A distinguished Georgia Freemason, W. Bro. Lee Hoyt Williams, now in his 85th year, was among other entitlements, Georgia Secretary of Quatuor Coronati Lodge 2076 until a few years ago. Even today he is one of the most enthusiastic members of The Masonic Book Club. One day he induced me, with no trouble at all, to seek membership in the Correspondence Circle of Quatuor Coronati Lodge 2076 of London. This led to some knowledge of and later personal acquaintance and friendship with W. Bro. Harry Carr, P.M., Secretary of the London lodge. Brother Carr, learning of my long quest for a copy of Preston, advised me of a possible source in London. My search was soon over.

This edition of Preston's *Illustrations of Masonry* is the crown jewel of my Masonic book collection. The opportunity to share this landmark book with my brethren of The Masonic Book Club is deeply appreciated.

WALTER M. CALLAWAY, JR.
Atlanta, Georgia, 1973

FACSIMILE PAGES

of

Illustrations of Masonry

ILLUSTRATIONS

OF

MASONRY.

The man, whose mind on virtue bent,
Pursues some greatly good intent
  With undiverted aim;
Serene, beholds the angry croud,
Nor can their clamours fierce and loud,
  His stubborn honour tame.
       BLACKLOCK.

The SECOND EDITION,
CORRECTED AND ENLARGED.

LONDON:

Printed for J. WILKIE, No. 71. St. Paul's Church Yard. MDCCLXXV.

TO THE
RIGHT HONOURABLE
LORD PETRE,
GRAND MASTER

OF THE

ANCIENT AND HONOURABLE SOCIETY

OF

FREE AND ACCEPTED MASONS,

THESE ILLUSTRATIONS

ARE, WITH THE GREATEST RESPECT,

INSCRIBED;

BY HIS LORDSHIP's

MOST OBEDIENT

SERVANT, AND BROTHER,

WILLIAM PRESTON.

The Sanction.

WHEREAS Brother WILLIAM PRESTON has compiled a Book, entitled, 'ILLUSTRATIONS OF MASONRY,' and has requested our Sanction for the publication thereof: we having perused the said Book, and finding it to correspond with the ancient practices of this Society, do recommend the same.

PETRE, Grand Master.
ROWLAND HOLT, D. G. M.
THOMAS NOEL, } G. Wardens.
JOHN HATCH,

JAMES HESELTINE,
   G. Secretary.

A Letter to Brother WILLIAM PRESTON.

Sir, and Brother,

The eminent service you have rendered to Masonry, by your late masterly work, has given us universal satisfaction, and demands our warmest acknowledgments: a performance, which, whilst it excites our gratitude, animates our zeal. We have *now* the happiness of seeing—what we always *hitherto* wished for, and lamented the want of, as the only remaining *desideratum* that we could hope for, or even desire;—the principles of our Ancient and Honourable Craft held up to mankind in so clear, perspicuous, and amiable a light, as the most enlightened must view with rapture, and even the most profane admire with reverence, awe, veneration, and esteem. It is in vain to multiply words. We cannot, we will not, compliment with the unmeaning prolixity of superfluous expressions: Much we might certainly say without deceit or flattery; but let *even* the *ceremonious* part of politeness give place in *our* words and actions to love, honour, harmony, and proportion.

With

With the sincerest and most affectionate thanks for your elegant publication, and the most sanguine expectations in every respect from your generous ardour and uncommon abilities, we beg leave to subscribe ourselves,

   Sir, and Brother,
    Your grateful Brethren, and
     Very obliged humble servants,
       STEP. BELL.
       M. ALLISON.
Falmouth,
Aug. 16th, 1773.   SAM. HIGMAN.

King's Arms Lodge, Die Mercurii, 28 Julii,
Falmouth, No. 116. A. L. 5773.

A lodge was this day held at the house of of Brother Edward Snoxell, (Brother Nicholas Symons, Master, in the chair) when a motion being made by Brother Stephen Bell, Deputy Provincial Grand Master, and seconded by Brother Matthew Allison, Provincial Secretary, the lodge came to the following resolutions, viz.

Resolved, That a letter of thanks be transmitted to Brother William Preston, for his very ingenious and elegant pamphlet, intitled " Illustrations of Masonry."

Resolved, That a committee, consisting of *three* members of this lodge, be appointed, in order to signify to Brother Preston the very great respect this lodge pays him as a Mason; and to communicate to him what sentiments it entertains of his publication.

Resolved, That Brother Stephen Bell, Deputy Provincial Grand Master, Brother M. Allison, Provincial Secretary, and Brother Sam. Higman, Secretary to this lodge, be the committee for conducting this business.

By Order of the Lodge,

SAM. HIGMAN, Secretary.

PREFACE.

Whoever confiders, with attention, the nature and defign of Mafonry, muft readily admit its general utility. Few of the members of this Society, who have examined its tenets, have ever retracted their favourable opinion of it. Did not its own excellence ftrike with immediate conviction, it never could have been fo ftrenuoufly fupported, fo nobly patronized, or fo greatly encouraged, through a long fucceffion of ages. Men of the moft diftinguifhed talents, and of the higheft rank, in all countries, have not difdained to lay afide thofe diftinctions to which their character in life entitle them; that they might enjoy the pleafures, and partake of the privileges, of Mafonry.

From a perfect fenfe of its utility, and an anxious defire to difplay its value, I have been induced to offer the following papers to the confideration of the Public.

PREFACE.

Many reasons might have withheld me from the attempt; my inability as a writer, my attention to the duties of my profession, and the many abler hands who have treated the subject before me: yet, under all these disadvantages, the persuasions of my friends, added to my zeal in the cause, have enabled me to surmount every difficulty, and to risk my reputation on the fate of my performance.

The favourable reception this Publication has met with in its first state, has induced me to spare no pains in rendering its second appearance in the world not less undeserving the attention of the brethren. This Edition contains many articles never before published, and is considerably enlarged by the addition of several useful remarks and observations. The principal articles are compiled from authentic records, and the best authorities I could procure. I have not always particularly specified the different sources of my information; because the facts I have adduced are well known to the majority of the brethren who are conversant with the ancient

cient practices of the Society. To my friends I am indebted for many extracts from old MSS. which tend to illustrate my subject, particularly to my worthy brother Capt. George Smith, Inspector of the Royal Academy at Woolwich, from whom I had the pleasure to receive many valuable annotations.

An account of the proceedings at the Grand Gala in 1772, as it was a temporary affair, I have entirely omitted, to make room for more useful matter. The oration which was delivered on that occasion I have included in the Vindication of Masonry, which I have divided into sections, that any particular part of it may occasionally be more easily referred to. In the illustration of the lectures, which constitutes the second part of this Edition, I have extended my remarks to all the degrees, and have introduced a concise description of certain particulars, which come under our consideration in the course of the different sections. To the Public, in general, these may appear rather unconnected and improperly placed, but to the well-informed mason, I flatter myself, they will be useful and interesting.

The historical part of the Work is considerably enlarged, and Masonry is traced from its first appearance in England to the present time. An account is given of the most remarkable occurrences of the Society, and of its patrons and protectors, at different periods. The detail of some of the civil commotions in the reign of Henry VI. which was given in the First Edition, I thought to have now omitted, but as it appears, from some old papers which have come under my inspection, that the edict issued at that time against the masons took its rise from a false suspicion of their being concerned in these disturbances, I have found it necessary still to retain the account. In order, however, not to interrupt the history in its regular course, I have given the chief part of these transactions in the notes.

At the end I have inserted a few songs, which I apprehend will be more necessary, as many of them may be introduced, with

propriety,

PREFACE.

propriety, to enliven the proceedings in the courfe of the ceremonies of which I have given an explanation.

In fhort, I have ufed my beft endeavours to render this Edition complete, but how I have fucceeded in my defign, I muft leave the fraternity to determine. It may be fufficient to obferve, that, as my intentions are good, I hope their candour and generofity will readily overlook any inaccuracies they may difcover; under the reflection, that my fubject would not admit of that open freedom of communication, which might have been expected from another theme, not under the fame reftrictions.

When I firft had the honour to be elected mafter of a lodge, I thought it my duty to inform myfelf more fully of the general rules of the Society; in order that I might be able to explain to the brethren under my direction, their utility and importance; and OFFICIALLY to enforce a due obedience to them. The various methods I adopted with this view, excited in fome of fuperficial knowledge, an absolute dislike, of what they considered as innovations; and in others of more enlarged faculties, a jealousy of pre-eminence, that the principles of Masonry ought to have checked. Notwithstanding these discouragements, I persevered in my intentions, of supporting the dignity of the Society, and of discharging with fidelity the trust reposed in me.

As candour and integrity, with a warm zeal, uninfluenced by interest and unbiassed by favour, will ever support a good cause, many of my opponents (pardon the expression) were soon convinced by argument of their error, and not only applauded my measures, but cheerfully concurred in their execution; while others secretly approved what their former declared opinions forbad them publicly to adopt.

This unexpected success exceeded my most sanguine wishes, and induced me to enquire, with a more minute attention, into the contents of our various lectures. The rude and imperfect state in which I found some of them, the difficulties I encountered in my search after others, and the variety

variety of modes established in our different assemblies, rather discouraged me in my first attempt: persevering, however, in my design, I continued my pursuit; and with a few zealous friends to the cause, who had carefully preserved what ignorance and the degeneracy of a corrupt age had rejected as unintelligible and absurd, I diligently sought for the ancient and venerable landmarks of the Society.

In the prosecution of my endeavours to revive the wise charges and useful regulations of Masonry, which inattention had suffered to sink into oblivion, I solicited the activity and assistance of my friends: And, with their kind help and generous support, I, in part, happily accomplished the design I had formed.

Directed by an assiduous study and careful perusal of our ancient charges, which we established as the basis of our work, our first step was attentively to consider the nature of the institution. To imprint on the memory their excellence and utility in the faithful discharge of our duty, we reduced the more material

rial parts of them into practice, and prosecuted our inquiries after still more useful knowledge.

To encourage others to join in our great undertaking, we observed a general rule of reading, or ordering to be read, one or other of these charges on every regular meeting; and of offering our sentiments in elucidation of such particular passages as seemed to be obscure. This practice we still retain, persuaded that a recital of our duty can never be disagreeable to those acquainted with it; and to those to whom it is not known, should any such be, it is highly proper to recommend it.

Such was the method we followed in the introduction of our plan, which being favourably received, we gradually improved, and brought into form the several sections which compose the three lectures of Masonry.

The progress made daily by our system, pointed out the necessity of obtaining the sanction of our patrons. Several of our brethren, gentlemen of acknowledged honour and integrity, joined with us in an application

application to the Grand Officers for their patronage; and the scheme of a Grand Gala * was proposed, as the most effectual means to convince them of the propriety of restoring Masonry to its primitive lustre, and rendering it worthy the attention of men of judgment and penetration. This happily succeeded, and the regularity observed by the officers in their different departments on the occasion, so fully answered the expectations of the original promoters, as not only to gain the sanction required, but to secure the countenance and support of our rulers to the prosecution of our plan.

I have thus ventured to appear in vindication of the ceremonies, and in support of the privileges of Masonry. If I continue to succeed in my expectations of giving the world a favourable idea of the institution, I shall be happy in the full completion of my wish. If my hopes are frustrated, I shall still indulge the not unpleasant reflection of having exerted my best endeavours in a good cause.

* The lecture on the first degree was publicly delivered on this occasion.

CONTENTS.

A Vindication of Masonry, including a Demonstration of its Excellency   1

Advertisement - - - 2

Sect. 1. Reflections on the symmetry and proportion displayed in the works of Nature, and throughout the various species of beings of every rank and all denominations - 3

§ 2. Friendship considered both in a limited and extended sense, and the advantages resulting from the exercise of this virtue - 7

§ 3. Few societies justly exempt from censure, but the attempts to slander Masonry vain   10

§ 4. Geometry the basis of Masonry; the great utility of this science to mankind - 13

§ 5. Masonry reconcilable to the best policy, and all men bound to promote it - 15

§ 6. Masonry considered under two denominations, operative and speculative - 17

§ 7. The government of the Society explained   19

§ 8. Reason assigned why the secrets of Masonry ought not to be publicly exposed - 22

§ 9. The

CONTENTS.

§ 9. The bad effects of the privilege of Masonry being indiscriminately bestowed, and the impropriety of considering the mysteries of the Order as slight and superficial - 23
§ 10. The good effects of preserving order and decorum in the lodges - 26
§ 11. The uniformity of opinion that prevails among Masons illustrated - 28
§ 12. The irregular lives of the professors of Masonry incompatible with the tenets of the Order - - - - 30
§ 11. Charity the distinguishing characteristic of Masons; that virtue explained - 32
§ 14. The discernment displayed by Masons in the proper choice of objects of charity 35
§ 15. Conclusion. Friendly admonitions 38
EULOGIUM - - - 41

Remarks on Masonry, including an Illustration of the Lectures, and a particular Description of several ancient ceremonies, &c. - - - 43
Advertisement - - - 44
General Remarks - - 45
Ceremony of opening and closing a Lodge 47
A Prayer used at opening the Lodge 49
——————————closing the Lodge 50
Laws at opening the Lodge - ib.
——————closing the Lodge - 53

CONTENTS.

Remarks on the FIRST LECTURE	56
Remark on the first section	57
———————— second section	58
Declaration of a candidate for Masonry	59
Proposition	60
Remark	ib.
Prayer at initiation into the First Degree	61
Remark on the third section	ib.
Charge at initiation into the First Degree	62
Remark on the fourth Section	68
The usages and customs among Masons similar to those of the ancient Egyptians	69
Remark on the fifth section	70
———————— sixth section	71
Brotherly love, relief, and truth explained	ib.
Cardinal virtues explained	73
General remarks on the SECOND LECTURE	75
Remark on the first section	77
Charge at initiation into the Second Degree	79
Remark on the second section	82
Orders in architecture explained	83
Five external senses explained	87
Remark on the third section	91
———————— fourth section	92
Seven liberal arts and sciences explained	93
The globes explained	96
General Remarks on the THIRD LECTURE	98
Remark on the first section	99

CONTENTS.

Remark on the second section	100
Prayer at initiation into the Third Degree	101
Charge at ditto	ib.
Remark on the third section	103
Remarks on the fourth, fifth, sixth, seventh, and eighth sections	104
Remarks on the ninth, tenth, eleventh, and twelfth sections	105
Ceremony of constitution	107
——————— consecration	111
——————— installation	113
——————— laying the foundation stones of public structures	128
——————— funerals	132
Funeral service	138
The Principles of Masonry explained in a Letter from Mr. Locke to the Earl of Pembroke	149
Advertisement	150
Old dialogue on Masonry	154
Glossary to ditto	164
Remarks on ditto	166
Remarks on secrecy	173
Instances of the great veneration paid to that art by the ancients	ib.
An entertaining story	174

CONTENTS.

History of Masonry in England	183
Advertisement	184
An account of the Druids	186
Progress of Masonry in England under the Romans	188
St. Alban procures a charter for the Masons from Carausius	190
St. Austin patronizes the Society	194
Alfred favours the Masons	196
Character of that Prince	197
Athelstane grants a charter to the Masons	198
——— falsely accused of murdering his brother Edwin	201
Masonry under the Grand Master of the Knights Templars	205
Edward III. a zealous patron of the Society	207
Extract from an old record in his reign	208
Act for abolishing the chapters of Masons	211
Judge Coke's opinion on that statute	212
Circumstances which gave rise to this act	214
Dr. Anderson's observation on this act	217
Civil commotions of this period	218
Duke of Gloucester murdered	225
Character of that Prince	226
Cardinal of Winchester's death, and anecdote concerning it	227
King Henry initiated into the Order, revises the constitutions, and patronizes the Lodges	228

History

CONTENTS.

History of Masonry in Scotland at this period 229
Masonry under the patronage of the Knights of
    Malta - - - 230
Queen Elizabeth sends an armed force to York,
    to break up the annual communications 233
Inigo Jones a zealous patron of the Masons 235
Extracts from Ashmole's diary - 237
Sir Christopher Wren presides over the frater-
    nity - - - 241
A short account of this architect - ib.
Revival of the Grand Lodge in 1717 246
Particular history of Masonry in England since
    that time - - - 248
Committee of charity established - 250
Provincial Grand Masters first appointed 253
Irregular assemblies of Masons censured, 258, 264
Dukes of Gloucester and Cumberland initiated
    266
Proposal for incorporating the Society, and build-
    ing a hall for the Grand Lodge - ib.
Remarks on the propriety of building a hall ib.
Description of the Banquetting Hall of the Lodge
    of St. John, at Marseilles - 267

Collection of Odes, Anthems, and Songs
    275
Advertisement - - - 276
Ode I. Hail to the Craft, &c. - 277
    II. Wake the lute, &c. - 278
                                Anthem

CONTENTS.

Anthem I.	Grant us, kind Heaven, &c.	279
II.	By Mason's art, &c.	280
Song I.	Arise, and blow thy trumpet,	ib.
II.	Unite, unite, &c.	281
III.	When earth's foundation, &c.	282
IV.	Genius of Masonry, &c.	283
V.	On, on, my dear Brethren, &c.	284
VI.	Hail Masonry, thou craft, &c.	285
VII.	Let Masonry from pole, &c.	287
VIII.	'Tis Masonry unites, &c.	ib.
IX.	Let Mason's fame resound,	289
X.	Hail Masonry divine, &c.	290
XI.	Let drunkards boast, &c.	291
XII.	Come let us prepare,	292
XIII.	To all who Masonry despise,	294
XIV.	Ye thrice happy few,	295
XV.	When a lodge of Free Masons,	297
XVI.	How happy a Mason, &c.	298
XVII.	When the sun from the East,	299

A

VINDICATION

OF

MASONRY,

INCLUDING

A Demonstration of its Excellency.

ADVERTISEMENT.

THE following Piece is founded on a Discourse composed by Brother CHARLES LESLIE, member of the Vernon Kilwinning Lodge, Edinburgh, and delivered by him at the consecration of that Lodge on the 15th of May, 1741. It was published in the Edinburgh Free-Masons Pocket Companion of the year 1765.

This ingenious author has displayed great taste in the choice of his subject, and has handled it with a considerable share of propriety. In building, however, on the foundation and the materials he has laid and collected, it appeared to me necessary to deviate in a great measure from his views; so that the superstructure I have raised is to be considered almost entirely as a new work.

The liberty I have taken, I hope will be freely pardoned, when it is remembered, that it proceeds from an ardent zeal to promote the reputation of a Society truly respectable.

A VINDICATION
OF
MASONRY.

WHOEVER reflects on the objects that surround him, will find abundant reason to admire the works of Nature, and adore the Being who directs such astonishing operations: he will be convinced, that infinite wisdom could alone design, and infinite power finish such amazing works.

If a man were placed in a beautiful garden, would not his mind, on a calm survey of its rich collections, be affected with the most exquisite delight? the groves, the grottoes, the artful wilds, the flowery parterres, the opening vistos, the lofty cascades, the winding streams, the whole variegated scene, would awaken his sensibility, and inspire his soul with the most exalted ideas. When he observed the delicate order, the nice symmetry, and beautiful disposition of every part, which though seemingly complete in itself, yet reflected surprising and new beauties on the other, so that nothing could be wanting to make one beautiful whole, with what bewitching sensations would his mind be agitated! A view of this delightful scene would naturally lead him to admire and venerate the happy genius of him who contrived it.

If the productions of art can so forcibly impress the human mind with surprise and admiration, with how much greater astonishment, and with what more profound reverence, must we behold the objects of Nature, which, on every hand, present to our view unbounded scenes of pleasure and delight, in which divinity and wisdom are alike conspicuous? The scenes which Nature displays are indeed
too

too expanded for the narrow capacity of man; yet it is eafy, from the uniformity of the whole, to comprehend what may lead to the true fource of happinefs, the grand Author of exiftence, the fupreme Governor of the world, the one perfect and unfullied Beauty.

Befide all the gaieties and pleafing profpects which every where furround us, and with which our fenfes are every moment gratified; befide the fymmetry, good order, and proportion, that appear in the whole works of the creation, there is fomething farther that affects the reflecting mind, and draws its attention nearer to the Divinity—the univerfal harmony and affection which fubfift throughout the different fpecies of beings of every rank and denomination. Thefe are the fure cements of the rational world, and by thefe alone the rational world fubfifts. Could we think that it was poffible for them to be diffolved, Nature too, and man, the chief work of God, would foon return to chaos, and univerfal ruin enfue.

If we look around us we shall find, that in the whole order of beings, from the seraph that adores and burns, down to the meanest insect, all, according to their proportion in the scale of existence, have, more or less, implanted in them by wise Nature, the principle of uniting with others of the same species with themselves. Do we not observe some of even the most inconsiderable animals formed into different ranks and societies for the benefit and protection of each other? Need I name the careful ant, or the industrious bee? insects which the wisest of men has recommended as a pattern of unwearied industry and prudent foresight.

If we raise our ideas higher, we shall find that the innate principle of friendship rises in proportion as the objects seem to advance nearer to the degree of rational. There can be no better way of judging of the superiority of one part of the animal creation above the other, than by observing what degrees of kindness and seeming good-nature they enjoy. However, I shall

shall here pause, and leave the disquisition of this philosophical subject to some more refined genius of superior abilities.

§ 2. No subject can more properly engage our attention, than the benevolent dispositions, and good temper of soul, which indulgent Nature has so kindly bestowed upon the rational species. These present to the mind agreeable reflections, and are replete with happy effects. The breast is inspired with tender feelings, and a reciprocal intercourse of kind and generous actions universally prevails. As human nature rises in the scale of things, so do the social affections likewise arise. When friendship is firm and cemented, we enjoy a high degree of pleasure; when it deadens or declines, we experience an equal degree of pain. In every breast there reigns a propensity to friendship, which, once properly established, sweetens every temporal enjoyment, and removes the disquietudes to which the infirmities of our nature expose us.

Friendship, in its progress through the circle of private connexions, gives rise to benevolence, which no limits can circumscribe. Its influence is universal, and extends to every branch of the human race. This virtue leads us to view the interest of society as the interest of each individual. Actuated by this principle, the same sentiments insensibly operate on the mind, and prompt us to seek our own happiness in the happiness of our fellow-creatures. Thus a fixed and permanent union is established among mankind.

Nevertheless, though the influence of friendship, considered as the source of benevolence, is unlimited, it exerts itself more or less vehemently as the objects it favours are nearer or more remote. Hence springs true patriotism, which fires the soul with the most generous flame, creates the best and most disinterested virtue, and inspires that public spirit and heroic ardor, which enables us to support a good cause, and risk our lives in its defence.

This commendable virtue crowns the lover of his country with unfading laurels, gives a luftre to all his actions, and confecrates his name to lateft ages. The warrior's glory may confift in murder, and the rude ravage of the defolating fword; but the blood of thoufands will not ftain the hands of his country's friend. His virtues are open, and of the nobleft kind. Confcious integrity fupports him againft the arm of power; and fhould he bleed by tyrant-hands, he glorioufly dies a martyr in the caufe of liberty, and leaves to pofterity an everlafting monument of the greatnefs of his foul.

Friendfhip not only appears divine when employed in preferving the liberties of our country, but fhines with equal fplendor in the more tranquil hours of life. Before it rifes into the noble flame of patriotifm, aiming deftruction at the heads of tyrants, thundering for liberty, and courting dangers in a good caufe; we fhall fee it calm and moderate, burning with an even glow, improving the foft hours of peace, and heightening the relish for virtue. Hence it is that contracts are formed, societies are instituted, and the vacant hours of life are cheerfully employed in agreeable company, and social conversation.

Though every man who carefully listens to the dictates of reason, may arrive at a clear persuasion of the necessity and beauty of virtue both private and public; yet it is a full recommendation of a society to have these pursuits continually in view as the sole objects of their association: and these are the laudable bonds that unite free-masons together in one indissoluble fraternity.

§ 3. Among the various kinds of societies to which the passions and inclinations of men have given birth, we find few that are justly exempt from censure. The influence of friendship seldom operates so powerfully in our general associations, as to promote that sincere attachment to the welfare and prosperity of each other, which can alone constitute the essence of civil society. This may
be

be attributed to several causes, but to no one with more propriety than to the reprehensible motives which generally lead us to the participation of social entertainments. It frequently happens, that in the quick circulation of the cheerful glass, we forget the more important duties of life, and bury our noblest faculties in the cup of ebriety. From such unguarded conduct the more prudent part of mankind have conceived a general prejudice against convivial meetings, of which it is difficult to wipe off the impression. Thus the best institutions may be brought into contempt by the indiscretion of those who form them.

Masonry has not escaped this general censure. Though by a secret and attractive force it disposes the heart to every social virtue, there are men so callous to every laudable principle, as to resist its influence, and even to act in direct contradiction to its best established rules. Hence the uninstructed part of mankind have been encouraged to cherish an indifferent idea of the institution, and ignorantly to propagate their opinions to the world. Thus the proceedings of a society which merits the highest encomiums, have been subjected to the most unjust aspersions. Vain, however, is each idle surmise against it; while Masonry is properly supported, it will be proof against every attack of its most inveterate enemies. Men are not aware, that by decrying laudable institutions, they derogate from the dignity of human nature, and from that good order and wise disposition of things which the almighty Author of the world has framed for the government of mankind, and has established as the basis of the moral system. Friendship and social delights can never be the object of reproach. That wisdom which hoary Time has sanctified, can never be the object of ridicule. Whoever pretends to censure or contemn what they cannot comprehend, must appear equally mean and contemptible. The generous heart will pity ignorance so aspiring and insolent.

§ 4. Geo-

§ 4. Geometry, the first and noblest of sciences, is the basis on which the superstructure of Masonry is erected. By geometry, we may curiously trace Nature through her various windings, to her most concealed recesses. By it we may discover the power, the wisdom, and the goodness of the grand Artificer of the universe, and view with amazing delight the beautiful proportions which connect and grace this vast machine. By it we may discover how the planets move in their different orbs, and mathematically demonstrate their various revolutions. By it we may rationally account for the return of seasons, and the mixed variety of scenes which they display to the discerning eye. Numberless worlds are around us, all framed by the same Divine Artist, which roll through the vast expanse, and are all conducted by the same unerring law of Nature. How must we then improve? With what grand ideas must such knowledge fill our minds; and how worthy is it of the attention of all rational beings?

A survey

A survey of nature, and the observation of its beautiful proportions, first determined man to imitate the divine plan, and to study symmetry and order. This gave rise to societies, and birth to every useful art. The architect began to design, and the plans which he laid down, improved by experience and time, produced some of those excellent works which will be the admiration of future ages.

Thus, from the commencement of the world, we may trace the foundation of Masonry. Ever since order began, and harmony displayed her charms, it has had a being. During many ages, and in many different countries, it has flourished. No art, no science preceded it. In the dark periods of antiquity, when literature was in a low state, and the rude manners of our forefathers withheld from them the knowledge we now so amply share, Masonry began to diffuse her influence. The mysteries of this science unveiled, arts
instantly

instantly arose, civilization took place, and the progress of knowledge and philosophy gradually dispelled the gloom of ignorance and barbarism. Government being settled, authority was given to laws, and the assemblies of the fraternity acquired the patronage of the great and the good, while the tenets of the profession were attended with general and unbounded utility.

§ 5. I shall now proceed to consider in what other respects Masonry is of universal utility to mankind, how it is reconcilable to the best policy, and why all men are bound to promote it. It is not my intention to enter into an elaborate disquisition of the institution; the task far exceeds my abilities; I shall only submit to the serious consideration of my readers a few general observations on the subject.

Abstracting from the pure pleasures which arise from a friendship so wisely constituted as that which subsists among masons,

masons, and which it is scarce possible that any circumstance or occurrence can erase, we find Masonry is a science confined to no particular country, but diffused over the whole terrestrial globe. Wherever arts flourish, there it flourishes too. Add to this, that by secret and inviolable signs, carefully preserved among the fraternity throughout the world, Masonry becomes an universal language. By this means, many advantages are gained: The distant Chinese, the wild Arab, or the American savage, will embrace a brother Briton; and he will know, that beside the common ties of humanity, there is still a stronger obligation to engage him to kind and friendly actions. The spirit of the fulminating priest will be tamed; and a moral brother, though of a different persuasion, engage his esteem. Thus all those disputes which embitter life and sour the tempers of men, are avoided; and every face is clad in smiles, while the common good of all, the general design of the craft, is zealously pursued.

Hence

Hence the univerſal utility of Maſonry is ſufficiently obvious. It unites men of the moſt oppoſite religions, of the moſt diſtant countries, and of the moſt contradictory opinions, in one indiſſoluble bond of unfeigned affection, and binds them, by the ſtrongeſt ties, to the practice of ſecrecy, morality, and virtue. Thus in every nation a maſon may find a friend, and in every climate he may find a home.

Is it not then evident, that Maſonry is an univerſal advantage to mankind? Unleſs diſcord and harmony be the ſame, it muſt be ſo. It is likewiſe reconcilable to the beſt policy, as it prevents that heat of paſſion and thoſe partial animoſities which different intereſts too often create.

§ 6. Maſonry paſſes and is underſtood under two denominations: it is operative and ſpeculative. By the former, we allude to the uſeful rules of architecture, whence a ſtructure derives figure, ſtrength, and beauty, and whence reſult a due proportion

portion and a just correspondence in all its parts. By the latter, we learn to subdue the passions, act upon the square, keep a tongue of good report, maintain secrecy, and practise charity.

Speculative Masonry is so much interwoven with religion, as to lay us under the strongest obligations to pay to the Deity that rational homage, which at once constitutes the duty and happiness of mankind. It leads the contemplative to view with reverence and admiration the glorious works of the creation, and inspires them with the most exalted ideas of the perfections of the great Creator.— Operative Masonry furnishes us with dwellings, and convenient shelters from the vicissitudes and the inclemencies of seasons. It displays human wisdom in a proper arrangement of materials, and demonstrates that a fund of science and industry is implanted in the rational species for the most wise, salutary, and beneficent purposes.

The

The lapse of time, the ruthless hand of ignorance, and the devastations of war, have laid waste and destroyed many valuable monuments of antiquity. Even the temple of king SOLOMON, so spacious and magnificent, and constructed by so many celebrated artists, was yet laid in ruins, and escaped not the unsparing ravages of barbarous force. Free-Masonry, notwithstanding, has been able still to survive. The attentive ear receives the sound from the instructive tongue, and its sacred mysteries are safely lodged in the repository of faithful breasts. The tools and implements of architecture, symbols the most expressive! imprint on the memory wise and serious truths, and transmit unimpaired, through the succession of ages, the excellent tenets of this institution.

§ 7. Masonry is a progressive science, and is divided into different classes or degrees, under particular restrictions and injunctions of fidelity, for the more regular

gular advancement of its profeffors in the knowledge of its myfteries. According to the progrefs we make, we are led to limit or extend our inquiries; and in proportion to our genius and capacity, we attain to a greater or lefs degree of perfection. This mode of government may fufficiently explain the importance of Mafonry, and give us a true idea of its nature and defign.

Three claffes are generally received under different appellations. The privileges of each are diftinct, and particular means are adopted to preferve thefe privileges to the juft and meritorious. Honour and probity are recommendations to the firft clafs, in which the practice of virtue is enforced, and the duties of morality inculcated; while the mind is prepared for focial converfe, and a regular progrefs into the principles of knowledge and philofophy. Diligence, affiduity, and application, are qualifications for the fecond clafs, in which an accurate elucidation of fcience, both in theory and practice,

OF MASONRY.

practice, is given; human reason is cultivated by a due exertion of our rational and intellectual powers and faculties; nice and difficult theories are explained; fresh discoveries are produced, and those already known are beautifully embellished. The third class is confined to a select few, whom truth and fidelity have distinguished, whom years and experience have improved, and whom merit and abilities have entitled to preferment. With them the ancient landmarks of the Order are preserved; and from them we learn and practise those necessary and instructive lessons which dignify the Art, and qualify its professors to convince the uninstructed of its excellence and utility.

This is our established mode of government when we act in conformity to our rules: hence true friendship is cultivated between different ranks and degrees of men, hospitality is promoted, industry rewarded, ingenuity encouraged, and all unnecessary distinctions are lost in the general good.

§ 8. If

§ 8. If the secrets of Masonry are replete with advantage to mankind, it may be asked, why is not the possession of them attended with better effects, and why are they not publickly exposed for the general good of society? To this it may be answered; if the privileges of Masonry were to be common, or indiscriminately bestowed, the design of the institution would not only be subverted, but being familiar, like many other important matters, they would soon lose their value, and sink into disregard.

It is a weakness in human nature, that men are generally more charmed with novelty, than the real worth or intrinsic value of things. The operations of Nature, though beautiful, magnificent, and useful, are frequently overlooked, because common and familiar. The sun rises and sets, the sea flows and reflows, rivers glide along their channels, trees and plants vegetate, men and beasts act, and all these, ever present to our eyes, yet remain unnoticed. The most astonishing productions

productions of nature are passed over with indifference on account of their familiarity, and excite not one single emotion, either in admiration of the great cause, or of gratitude for the blessings conferred. Even virtue itself is not exempted from this unhappy bias in the constitution of the human frame. Novelty influences all our actions, all our determinations. Every thing that is new or difficult in the acquisition, however trifling or insignificant, readily captivates the imagination, and ensures a temporary admiration; while what is familiar, or easily attained, however noble or eminent for utility, is sure to be disregarded by the giddy and the unthinking.

§ 9. It is a truth too obvious to be concealed, that the privileges of Masonry have been too common. Hence we may assign a reason why their good effects are not more conspicuous.—Several persons enrol their names in our records merely to oblige their friends; and reflect

flect not on the confequences of fuch a meafure, nor inquire into the nature of their particular engagements. Not a few are prompted by motives of intereft; and many are introduced with no better view than to pleafe as good companions. A general odium, or at leaft a carelefs indifference, is the refult of fuch conduct.—But here the evil ftops not.—Thefe perfons, ignorant of our noble principles, probably without any real defect in their own morals, are led to recommend others of the fame caft with themfelves for the fame purpofe. Thus, behold the end! the moft facred part of Mafonry is turned into fcoff and ridicule, and the fuperficial practices of a luxurious age bury in oblivion principles which have dignified princes, and the moft exalted characters.

If our fecrets or peculiar forms conftituted the effence of the art, it might with fome degree of propriety be alleged that our amufements were trifling, and our ceremonies abfurd. But this the fkilful well-informed mafon knows to be falfe. He draws them to a nearer inspection; he adverts to the circumstances which gave rise to them; he considers and dwells upon the excellent lessons they inculcate; and finding them replete with useful knowledge, he adopts them as keys to our privileges, and prizes them as sacred. Thus he is convinced of the propriety of our solemnities, and candidly acknowledges their value from their utility.

Many have been deluded by the vague supposition that the mysteries of Masonry were merely nominal, that the practices established among us were slight and superficial, and that our ceremonies were of such trifling import, as to be adopted or waved at pleasure. Establishing their opinion on this false foundation, we have found them hurrying through all the degrees without adverting to the necessary qualifications. Having passed through the usual formalities, they have accepted offices, and assumed the government of Lodges, equally unacquainted with the duties of the trusts reposed in them, and the design of the society they pretended to govern. The consequence is obvious; anarchy and confusion have ensued, and the substance has been lost in the shadow.— Thus men eminent for ability, for rank, and for fortune, view with indifference the distinguished honours of Masonry, and either accept offices with reluctance, or reject them with disdain.

Such are the disadvantages under which our society has long laboured. Every zealous friend to Masonry must earnestly wish for a reformation of these abuses. Of late years, to the honour of our present patrons, let it be acknowledged, that under their auspices our assemblies have been better regulated.

§ 10. The good effects of preserving order and decorum, promoting harmony, and inculcating a due obedience to the general regulations of the Order are too obvious to require a laboured elucidation. Of this the flourishing state of several Lodges who have adopted a regular plan of government, are convincing proofs. If the brethren who have the honour to preside over Lodges, were properly apprized of the duties of their respective offices, a general reformation would soon take place. This hint may probably be productive of good consequences, as a step so laudable must evince the propriety of our several appointments, and lead mankind to acknowledge, that sometimes at least our honours are deservedly bestowed. Thus the ancient lustre of our respectable fraternity will be happily restored, and our system of government universally applauded; virtue being duly encouraged, and merit properly rewarded.

This conduct can alone retrieve our character. Our prudent actions must distinguish our title to the honours of Masonry, and our regular deportment display the influence and utility of our excellent rules. The world in general will then admire the regularity of our measures, and reconcile the uniformity of our proceedings with the tenets we profess to revere.

§ 11. Masonry is founded upon harmony, and subsists by regularity and proportion. The delicate pleasures of friendship harmonize our minds, and exclude rancour, malice, or ill-nature. We cultivate brotherly love, and reconcile ourselves to the practice of every amiable virtue. By improving the mind in the principles of morality, we enlarge our understandings, and more effectually answer the great ends of our existence.

No estrangement of behaviour is observed in our assemblies. An uniformity of opinion, not only useful in exigencies, but pleasing in familiar life, universally prevails among us, strengthens all the ties of our friendship, and equally promotes love and esteem. Masons are brethren by a double tie, and among brothers there can exist no invidious distinctions. A king is reminded, that although a crown adorns his head, and a sceptre his hand,

hand, yet the blood in his veins is derived from the common parent of mankind, and is no better than that of the meanest of his subjects. Men in inferior stations are taught to love their superiors, when they see them divested of their grandeur, and condescending to trace the paths of wisdom, and follow virtue, assisted by those of a rank beneath them. Virtue is true nobility, and wisdom is the channel by which it is directed and conveyed. Wisdom and virtue alone distinguish masons.

Masonry, therefore, of itself, commands the highest regard, claims the greatest esteem, and merits the most extensive patronage. If all that is good and amiable, if all that is useful to mankind or society, be deserving a wise man's attention, Masonry claims it in the highest degree. It inspires beautiful ideas, opens and enlarges the mind, and affords an abundant source of satisfaction. It recommends universal benevolence, and every virtue which can endear one man to another; and is particularly adapted to give the mind the most disinterested, the most generous notions.

Such is the nature of our venerable institution. Union is cemented by sincere attachment, hypocrisy and deceit are unknown, and pleasure is reciprocally communicated by the cheerful observance of every obliging office. Virtue, the grand object in view, luminous as the meridian sun, shines refulgent on the mind, enlivens the heart, and converts cool approbation into warm sympathy and cordial attention.

§ 12. If the preceding account of Masonry be not exaggerated, it may excite surprise, why so few of its professors are distinguished for exemplary lives. When we consider the variety of members of which the society consists, and the small number of those who are conversant with the tenets of the institution, our wonder will, in some degree, abate. It must be admitted, that though the fairest and best ideas may be imprinted on the mind, there are some persons, who, careless of their own reputation, will consequently disregard the most instructive lessons. Such, I am sorry to observe, are sometimes to be found among the professors of Masonry. Many, even distinguished for a knowledge of the Art, are often disposed to violate those rules, to which a pretended conformity may have gained them applause. By yielding to vice and intemperance, they frequently not only disgrace themselves, but reflect dishonour upon Masonry in general. This unfortunate circumstance has given rise to many severe reflections, which the prejudiced part of mankind have liberally bestowed upon the society. But let it be proclaimed to the world at large, that these apostates are unworthy of their trust, and that, whatever name or designation they assume, they are in reality *no* masons. It is equally incompatible with the tenets of Masonry and the engagements of its professors, to commit a dishonourable action. Masonry consists in virtuous improvement, in cheerful and innocent pastime, and not in lewd debauchery or unguarded excefs.

But though unhappy brethren thus tranfgrefs, no wife man will draw any argument from thence againft the fociety, or urge it as an objection againft the inftitution. If the wicked lives of men were admitted as an argument againft the religion which they profefs, chriftianity itfelf, with all its divine beauties, would be expofed to cenfure.

Thus much we may aver in favour of Mafonry, that it countenances an error in no individual. Such as violate our laws, or infringe on good order, are marked with a peculiar odium; and if our mild endeavours to reform their lives fhould not anfwer the good purpofes intended, they are expelled our affemblies, as unfit members of fociety. Thus we fupport the dignity of our character, and difplay Mafonry in its genuine luftre.

§ 13. Charity is the chief of every focial virtue, and the diftinguifhing characteriftic of our order. This virtue not only

only includes a supreme degree of love to the great Creator and Governor of the universe, but an unlimited affection to beings of all characters and of every denomination. This last duty is forcibly inculcated by the example of the Deity himself, who liberally dispenses his beneficence to unnumbered worlds.

The bounds of the greatest nation or the most extensive empire cannot circumscribe the generosity of a liberal mind. Mankind, in whatever situation they are placed, are still, in a great measure, the same. They are exposed to similar dangers and misfortunes. They have not wisdom to foresee, or power to prevent, the evils incident to their nature. They hang in perpetual suspense betwixt hope and fear, sickness and health, plenty and want. A mutual chain of dependence subsists throughout the animal creation. The whole human species are therefore proper objects for the exercise of charity. Beings who partake of one common nature, ought ever to be

actuated

actuated by the same motives and interests. Hence, to sooth the unhappy, by sympathizing with their misfortunes, and to restore peace and tranquillity to agitated spirits, constitute the general and great ends of our institution. This humane, this generous disposition, fires the breast with the most manly feelings, and enlivens that spirit of compassion, which is the glory of the human frame, and which not only rivals, but outshines every other pleasure the mind is capable of enjoying.

All human passions, if directed by the superior principle of reason, tend to promote some useful purpose; but compassion exerted on proper objects, is the most beneficial of all other affections; it extends to greater numbers, and excites more lasting degrees of happiness.

Possessed of this amiable, this godlike disposition, we are shocked at misery under every form and appearance. The healing accents that flow from our tongue, not only alleviate the pain of the unhappy sufferer,

sufferer, but make even adversity, in her dismal state, look gay. Our pity excited, we assuage grief, and cheerfully relieve distress. When a brother is in want, every heart is prone to ache; when he is hungry, we convey him food; when he is naked, we clothe him; and when he is in trouble, we fly to his relief. Thus we evince the propriety of the title we assume, and demonstrate to the world that the term BROTHER among masons is not merely a name.

If these acts are not sufficient to recommend so great and generous a plan, such a wise and good society, happy in themselves, and equally happy in the possession of every social virtue, nothing which is truly good can prevail. The man who resists arguments drawn from such topics, must be lost to all sense of honour, and callous to the noblest principles.

§ 14. It must be acknowledged by the most inveterate enemies of Masonry, that no society is more remarkable for the practice of charity, nor any assembly of men more universally famed for disinterested liberality. It cannot be said that we meet only in order to indulge in convivial mirth, while the poor and needy pine for relief. Our quarterly distributions, exclusive of the private subscriptions in our different lodges, to relieve distress, will prove the contrary. We are always ready, in proportion to our circumstances, cheerfully to contribute to alleviate the misfortunes of our fellow-creatures. When we consider, however, the variety of persons who present themselves at our several meetings, whose seeming distress the dictates of Nature as well as the ties of Masonry incline us to pity and relieve, we find it necessary sometimes to inquire into the cause of their misfortunes; lest a misconceived tenderness of disposition, or an impolitic generosity of heart, should prevent our making a proper distinction in the choice of objects. Though our hearts and ears are ever impressed with, and open to the distresses of the deserving poor, yet our charity is not to be misapplied, nor our bounty dispensed with a profuse liberality on those who may probably use Masonry as a cloak to cover their impostures. Those who are burdened with a numerous offspring, and through age, sickness, infirmity, or some unforeseen accident in life, are reduced to poverty and want, particularly claim our attention, and seldom fail to experience the happy effects of our fraternal associations. We consider their situation as more easy to be conceived than expressed, and are induced liberally to extend our charity in their behalf. Thus we give convincing proofs of our wisdom and discernment; for though our benevolence is, as our laws, unlimited, yet our hearts glow principally with affection toward the deserving part of mankind.

From the above view of the advantages resulting from the practice and profession of Masonry, it is evident every candid and

and impartial person must acknowledge its superiority to the greater part of modern institutions. It is then surely no mean advantage, no trifling acquisition to any government or state, to have under its jurisdiction a society of men who are loyal subjects, patrons of science, and friends to mankind.

§ 15. Having explained the principles of Masonry, and endeavoured to demonstrate its excellence and utility, I shall conclude my observations with a few friendly admonitions, which I hope will be favourably received, as they proceed from a zealous attachment to the society.

As useful knowledge is the great object of our desire, let us with assiduity apply to the practice and profession of Masonry. The ways of wisdom are beautiful, and lead to pleasure. Knowledge must be attained by degrees, and is not every where to be found. Wisdom seeks the secret shade, the lonely cell designed for contemplation. There enthroned she sits, delivering her sacred oracles. There let us seek her, and pursue the real bliss. Though the passage is difficult, the farther we trace it, the easier it will become.

If we are united, our society must flourish. Let all private animosities, if any should exist, give place to peace and good fellowship. Uniting in the grand design, let us be happy ourselves, and endeavour to contribute to the happiness of others. Let us promote the useful arts, and by that means mark our superiority and distinction; let us cultivate the social virtues, and improve in all that is good and amiable; let the genius of Masonry preside, and under her sovereign sway let us endeavour to act with becoming dignity. On every occasion let us preserve a nobleness and justness of understanding, a politeness of manner, and an evenness of temper. Let our recreations be innocent and pursued with moderation,

deration, and never let us suffer irregular indulgences to expose our character to derision. Thus our conduct will be conformable to our precepts, and we shall support the name we have always borne, of being the most respectable, the most regular, and the most uniform society under the Sun.

EULO.

EULOGIUM.

Masonry ftamps an indelible mark of pre-eminence on all its profeffors, which neither chance, power, nor fortune can beftow on thofe who have not been initiated into its myfteries. It is a fure foundation of tranquillity amidft all the difappointments of life; it is a friend who will not deceive, but will comfort and affift, both in profperity and adverfity; it is a bleffing which will remain with all times, circumftances, and places, and may be had recourfe to when all other earthly comforts fail.

Mafonry gives real and intrinfic excellence to man, and renders him fit for the duties of focial life. It calms domeftic ftrife, is company in folitude, and gives vivacity, variety, and energy to focial converfation. In youth, it calms the paffions, and employs ufefully our moft active faculties; and in old age, when

ficknefs,

sickness, imbecillity and disease have benumbed every corporeal sense, and rendered the union of soul and body almost intolerable, it yields an inexhaustible fund of comfort and satisfaction.

Such are the general advantages of Masonry; to enumerate them separately, would be an endless labour: it may be sufficient to say, that he who is possessed of this true science, and acts agreeably to the character he bears, has within himself the spring and support of every social virtue; a subject of contemplation that enlarges the mind, and expands every mental power; a subject that is inexhaustible, is ever new, and always interesting.

REMARKS
ON
MASONRY,

INCLUDING

An ILLUSTRATION of the LECTURES, and a particular Description of several ancient Ceremonies;

TOGETHER WITH THE

CHARGES of the different Degrees, &c.

ADVERTISEMENT.

IN the First Edition, the Remarks on Masonry were confined to the First Lecture, as more immediately connected with the proceedings at the Grand Gala, with a description of which that Edition commenced. But as the Gala was a temporary affair, the description of it is now omitted, to make room for matter more generally useful; and the Remarks are extended to all the Degrees.

REMARKS

ON

MASONRY.

Masonry is justly considered as an art equally useful and extensive. It must be allowed, that in all arts there is a mystery; which requires a gradual progression of knowledge to attain to any degree of perfection in them. Without much instruction, and more exercise, no man can be skilful in any art; in like manner, without an assiduous application to the various sections comprehended in the different lectures of Masonry, no person can be sufficiently acquainted with its true value.

It is not, however, to be inferred from this remark, that persons who labour under the disadvantages of a confined education,

education, or whose sphere of life requires a more intense application to business or study, should be discouraged in their endeavours to gain a knowledge of Masonry. To qualify an individual to enjoy the benefits of the society, and to partake of its privileges, it is not absolutely necessary to be acquainted with the more intricate parts of the science. These are reserved only for the diligent and assiduous mason.

Some are more dextrous and artificial than others, some more expert, some more eminent, some more useful; yet all, in their different spheres, may prove advantageous to the community; and our necessities as well as our consciences bind us to love one another. It is certain that the industrious tradesman proves himself a very useful member of society, and worthy of every honour we can confer; yet still it must be allowed, that those who, by accepting offices, exercise authority, should be properly qualified to discharge it with honour to themselves, and credit to their different stations.—All men are

not

not bleſſed with the ſame powers, all men have not the ſame advantages: All men therefore are not equally qualified to govern.—Maſonry is founded upon too noble, too generous principles, to admit of diſquietude and variance among its profeſſors on that account; neither arrogance and preſumption appear on the one hand, nor diffidence and inability on the other. In the whole ſeries of our proceedings true friendſhip is cultivated among the different ranks of men, and that endearing happineſs promoted, which conſtitutes the eſſence of civil ſociety.

The Ceremony of opening and cloſing a Lodge.

In every regular aſſembly of men, who are convened for wiſe and uſeful purpoſes, the commencement and termination of buſineſs is attended with ſome form. Though ceremonies are in themſelves of little importance, yet as they ſerve to engage the attention, and to impreſs the mind with reverence, they muſt be conſidered as neceſſary

necessary on solemn occasions. They recall to memory the intent of the association, and banish many of those trifling amusements which too frequently intrude on our less serious moments.

From the most remote period of antiquity this practice may be traced. Being founded on a rational basis, the custom still prevails in every civilized country of the world.

The veneration due to antiquity, setting aside the reasonableness of the practice, would recommend it. To enlarge on the propriety of observing it in this society, which has received the sanction of the early ages, as well as the patronage of the wisest men in more recent periods, would, we apprehend, be equally needless and unimportant. As the custom is universally admitted among masons, we will proceed to consider the advantages of it, as far as the ties of the society will admit.

The ceremony used at the opening of our assemblies answers two purposes; it reminds the Master of the dignity of his character,

character, and the brethren of fidelity to their trust. These are not the only advantages resulting from it; a reverential awe for the Deity is inculcated. Here we are taught to adore the God who made us, and to supplicate his protection on our well-meant endeavours.

The closing of our meetings teaches us to offer up the proper tribute of gratitude to the beneficent Author of life; and here the less important duties of the society are not passed over unobserved. By this ceremony we are taught how to support the regularity of our assemblies, and the necessary degree of subordination which takes place in the government of our lodges.

Such is the nature and utility of this ceremony, that it becomes our duty never to omit it; hence it is arranged as a section in every degree of Masonry, and takes the lead in all our illustrations.

A Prayer used at opening the Lodge.

May the favour of Heaven be upon this our happy meeting; may it be begun, carried

carried on, and ended with order, harmony, and brotherly love. Amen.

A Prayer used at closing the Lodge.

May the blessing of Heaven be with us, and all regular masons; to beautify and cement us with every moral and social virtue. Amen.

A rehearsal of the ancient charges of the society properly succeeds the opening, and precedes the closing, of the lodge; we shall therefore give them in their due arrangement. The practice of explaining the original laws of Masonry ought not to be neglected in our regular assemblies. A repetition of our duty can never be disagreeable to those who are acquainted with it, and to those to whom it is not known, should any such be, it is highly proper to recommend it.

Management of the Craft in working.

[To be rehearsed at opening the Lodge.]

Masons employ themselves diligently in their sundry vocations, live creditably, and

and conform with cheerfulness to the laws and customs of the country in which they reside.

The most expert Craftsman is chosen or appointed Master of the work, and is duly honoured as such by those over whom he presides.

The Master knowing himself qualified, undertakes the government of the Lodge, and truly dispenses his rewards, giving to every brother the approbation he merits.

A Craftsman appointed Warden of the work under the Master, is true to both Master and fellows, carefully oversees the work, and his brethren obey him.

The Master, Wardens, and brethren receive their rewards justly, are faithful, and honestly finish the work they begin, whether it is in the first or second degree; but never put that work to the first, which has been accustomed to the second degree.

Neither envy nor censure is discovered among masons. No brother is supplanted, or put out of his work, if he is capable to finish the same; as no man can finish the work of another so much to the advantage of the Master, unless he is perfectly skilled in the original design.

All employed in Masonry meekly receive their rewards, and use no disobliging name. Brother or Fellow are the terms or appellations they bestow on each other. They behave courteously within and without the Lodge, and never desert the Master till the work is finished.

Laws for the Government of the Lodge.

You are to salute one another in a courteous manner, agreeably to the forms established among masons; you are freely to give such mutual instruction as shall be thought necessary or expedient, not being overseen or overheard, without encroaching upon each other, or derogating from that respect which is due to any gentleman were he not a mason; for though as masons we rank as brethren on a level, yet Masonry deprives no man of the honour due to his rank or character, but rather adds to his honour,

honour, especially if he has deserved well of the fraternity, who always render honour to whom it is due, and avoid ill manners.

No private committees are to be allowed, or separate conversation encouraged, the Master or Wardens are not to be interrupted, or any brother speaking to the Master; but the brethren are to observe due decorum, and under no pretence to use any unbecoming language, but pay a proper deference and respect to the presiding officers.

These laws are to be strictly enforced, that harmony may be preserved, and the business of the Lodge be carried on with order and regularity.

Amen. So mote it be.

Charge on the Behaviour of Masons.
[To be rehearsed at closing the Lodge.]

When the Lodge is closed, you may enjoy yourselves with innocent mirth; but you are carefully to avoid excess. You are not to compel any brother to act contrary to his inclination, or to give offence by word or deed, but enjoy a free and easy conversation. You are to use no immoral or obscene discourse, but support with propriety the dignity of your character.

You are to be cautious in your words and carriage, that the most penetrating stranger may not be able to discover, or find out, what is not proper to be intimated; and, if necessary, you are to divert the discourse, and manage it prudently, for the honour of the fraternity.

At home, and in your several neighbourhoods, you are to behave as wise and moral men. You are never to communicate to your families, friends or acquaintance, the private transactions of our different assemblies; but upon every occasion to consult your own honour, and the reputation of the society at large.

You are to study the preservation of your healths, by avoiding irregularity and intemperance, lest your families are neglected and injured, or yourselves disabled from

ON MASONRY.

from attending to your neceffary employments.

If a ftrange brother applies in that character, you are cautioufly to examine him in fuch a method as prudence may direct, and agreeably to the forms eftablifhed among mafons; that you may not be impofed upon by an ignorant falfe pretender, whom you are to reject with contempt, and beware of giving him any hints of knowledge. But if you difcover him to be a true and genuine brother, you are to refpect him accordingly: if he is in want, you are to relieve him, or direct him how he may be relieved; you are to employ him, or recommend him to be employed: however, you are never charged to do beyond your ability; only to prefer a poor brother, who is a good man and true, before any other perfon in the fame circumftances.

Finally, Thefe rules you are always to obferve and enforce, and alfo thofe duties which have been communicated in the lecture; cultivating brotherly love, the foundation

dation and capeſtone, the cement and glory of this ancient fraternity; avoiding, upon every occaſion, wrangling and quarrelling, ſlander and backbiting; not permitting others to ſlander your honeſt brethren, but defending their characters, and doing them all good offices, as far as may be conſiſtent with your honour and ſafety, but no farther. Hence all may ſee the benign influence of Maſonry, as all true maſons have done from the beginning of the world, and will do to the end of time.

Amen. So mote it be.

FIRST LECTURE.

Having illuſtrated the ceremony of opening and cloſing a Lodge, and inſerted the Charges and Prayers uſually rehearſed in our regular aſſemblies on both theſe occaſions, it will now be proper to enter on a particular diſquiſition of the contents of the Lectures appropriated to the different

ferent Degrees of Masonry, and give a brief summary of the whole, annexing to the Remarks on each section the particulars to which it alludes. By this means the industrious mason will be properly instructed in the arrangement of the sections in each lecture, and be thereby enabled with greater ease to acquire a knowledge of the Art.

The first lecture of Masonry paints virtue in the most beautiful colours, and enforces the duties of morality. In it we are taught such useful lessons as prepare our minds for a regular progress in the principles of knowledge and philosophy. These are imprinted on the memory by lively and sensible images, to influence our conduct in the proper discharge of the duties of social life.

The First Section.

The first section of this degree is suited to all capacities, and may and ought to be known to every mason who wishes to rank as a member of this society. It consists

… REMARKS

of general heads, which, though short and simple, yet carry weight along with them; and serve not only as marks of distinction, but communicate useful and interesting knowledge when duly examined. They qualify us to try and examine the rights of others to our privileges, while they prove our own; and as they induce us to inquire more minutely into other particulars of greater importance, they serve as an introduction to topics more amply elucidated in the following sections.

We can annex to this Remark no other explanation, consistent with the rules of Masonry; we shall therefore refer the more inquisitive to our regular assemblies for farther instruction.

The Second Section.

The second section makes us not only acquainted with our peculiar forms and ceremonies, but convinces us, beyond the power of contradiction, of the propriety of our solemnities; and demonstrates to
the

the most sceptical and hesitating mind, their excellence and utility.

As we are taught in this section the ceremony of initiation into the Order, the following particulars relative to that ceremony may be here introduced with propriety.

A Declaration to be assented to by every Candidate, previous to his being proposed.

Do you seriously declare, upon your honour, before these gentlemen*, that, unbiassed by friends and uninfluenced by mercenary motives, you freely and voluntarily offer yourself a candidate for the mysteries of Masonry?

Do you seriously declare, upon your honour, before these gentlemen, that you are solely prompted by a favourable opinion conceived of the institution, a desire of knowledge, and a sincere wish of being serviceable to your fellow-creatures?

---

* The Stewards of the Lodge.

Do you seriously declare, upon your honour, before these gentlemen, that you will cheerfully conform to all the ancient established usages and customs of the society?

When the above declaration is made, the candidate is then proposed in open Lodge, in manner following.

Proposition.

R. W. Master and brethren,

At the earnest request of Mr. A. B. [*mentioning his profession and residence,*] I propose him as a candidate for our mysteries. From a knowledge of his character, I recommend him as worthy to partake of the privileges of Masonry; and in consequence of a declaration of his intentions, just made, and properly attested, I firmly believe he will cheerfully conform to all the rules of this society.

[*Note.* It is a duty incumbent on every Master of a Lodge, previous to the initiation of a candidate into Masonry, to inform him of the purpose and design of the institution; to explain the nature of his solemn engagements; and, in a manner peculiar to masons alone, to require his cheerful acquiescence to the duties of morality and virtue, and all the sacred tenets of the Order.]

A Prayer used at the Initiation of a Candidate.

Vouchsafe thy aid, Almighty Father and supreme Governor of the world, to this our present convention; and grant that this candidate for Masonry may dedicate and devote his life to thy service, and become a true and faithful brother among us. Endue him with a competence of thy divine wisdom, that, by the secrets of this Art, he may be better enabled to unfold the mysteries of godliness, to the honour of thy holy name. Amen.

The Third Section.

The third section proves us to be regular members of the society, and inculcates those

those necessary and instructive duties, which at once dignify our characters in the double capacity of men and masons.

We cannot better illustrate the contents of this section, than by inserting the following charge:

Charge at Initiation into the First Degree *.

BROTHER,

[As you are now introduced into the first principles of our Royal Order, I have the pleasure to congratulate you on being accepted a Member of this most ancient and honourable Society: ancient, as having subsisted from time immemorial; and honourable, as tending, in every particular, to render all men so, who will be but conformable to its precepts. No society was ever raised on a better principle or more solid foundation; nor were ever more excellent rules and

---

* The paragraphs inclosed in brackets [ ] may be occasionally omitted, if time will not admit of delivering the whole Charge.

useful

useful maxims laid down, than are inculcated on all persons when initiated into the mysteries of this science. Monarchs, in all ages, have been encouragers and promoters of this Art, and have never deemed it derogatory from their dignity to level themselves with the fraternity, to extend their privileges, and to patronize their assemblies.]

As a gentleman and a mason you are bound to be a strict observer of the moral law, as contained in this holy book * ; to consider it as the unerring standard of truth and justice, and to regulate your life and actions by its divine precepts. Herein your duty to God †, to your neighbour ‡, and to yourself §, is duly inculcated; and

---

* The Bible.

† In never mentioning his name, but with that awe and respect which is due from a creature to his creator; to implore his aid in all your undertakings, and to esteem him as the chief good.

‡ In acting upon the square, and doing to him as you wish he should do to you.

§ In avoiding all irregularity and intemperance, unbecoming the dignity of human nature.

your zealous attachment to thefe duties will fecure both public and private efteem.

In the ftate, you are to be a quiet and peaceable fubject, true to your fovereign, and juft to your country; never to countenance difloyalty or rebellion, but patiently to fubmit to magifterial authority, and conform with cheerfulnefs to the government of the kingdom in which you live.

[In your outward demeanour you are to be particularly careful to avoid cenfure or reproach; and to beware of all thofe who may artfully endeavour to infinuate themfelves into your efteem, with a view to betray your virtuous refolutions, or make you fwerve from the honourable principles of this inftitution. Let not intereft, favour, or prejudice, ever bias your integrity, or influence you to be guilty of a difhonourable action; but let the whole feries of your conduct and behaviour be regular and uniform, and your deportment fuitable to the dignity of this laudable profeffion.]

Above all other virtues, practise benevolence and charity; two of the most distinguishing characteristics of this venerable institution. [The inconceivable pleasure of contributing towards the relief of our fellow-creatures can only be experienced by persons of a humane disposition; who are naturally excited, by the power of sympathy to extend their aid in alleviation of the miseries of others. This alone encourages the generous soul to distribute his bounty with cheerfulness. By supposing himself in their unhappy situation, he listens to their complaints with attention, bewails their misfortunes, and speedily relieves their distress.]

The next object of your attention, and which more immediately relates to your present state, is our excellent Book of Constitutions. It contains the history of Masonry from the earliest periods, with a list of the noble personages who have enriched the Art from ADAM to the present æra; and also the laws and regulations of the society.

A punctual

A punctual attendance on our assemblies is required, more especially on the duties of this lodge. Here, as in all other regular meetings of the fraternity, you are to behave with due order and decorum, that harmony may be preserved, and the business of the society be properly conducted. [You are not to lay, or offer to lay, wagers; nor use any unbecoming language in derogation of the name of God, or towards the corruption of good manners; neither are you to introduce, support, or maintain any dispute about religion or politics; nor to behave yourself ludicrously while the lodge is engaged in what is serious and important; but to pay a proper deference and respect to the Master and presiding officers, and diligently to apply to your work in Masonry, that you may the sooner become a proficient therein, as well for your own reputation, as the honour of the lodge in which you have been made.]

However, although your frequent appearance at our regular meetings is earnestly neftly folicited, yet Mafonry is not to interfere with your neceffary avocations; for thefe are on no occafion to be neglected. At your leifure hours you are required to ftudy the liberal arts and fciences; and, by that means, with a few private inftructions, you will foon attain a competent knowledge of our myfteries.

To conclude, you are to keep inviolable every particular inftruction of this folemn charge; and if ever, in the circle of your acquaintance, you fhould find one defirous of being accepted among mafons, you muft be particularly attentive not to recommend him, unlefs you are convinced he will conform to thefe rules; in order that the honour, glory, and reputation of this noble inftitution may be firmly eftablifhed, and the popular world be fully convinced of its benign influence.

[From the apparent attention you have paid to the recital of thefe duties, it is hoped that you will eftimate their real value, and ever imprint on your mind

the

the sacred dictates of truth, honour, and justice.]

The Fourth Section.

The fourth section rationally accounts for the origin of our hieroglyphics, and convinces us of the advantages which ever accompany a faithful observance of our duty; it illustrates at the same time certain particulars, of which our ignorance may lead us into error, and which as masons we are indispensably bound to know.

To make a daily progress in Masonry is a duty incumbent on every member of this society, and is expressly required by our general laws. What end can be more noble than the pursuit of virtue; what motive more alluring than the practice of justice; or what instruction more beneficial than an accurate elucidation of symbolical mysteries, which tend to embellish and adorn the human mind? Every thing that strikes the eye more immediately

ately engages the attention, and imprints on the memory thofe circumftances which are accompanied with ferious and folemn truths. Hence mafons have univerfally adopted the method of inculcating the tenets of their Order by typical figures and allegorical emblems. This practice has fecured their myfteries from defcending into the familiar reach of every inattentive and unprepared novice, from whom they might not receive due veneration.

The records of the fraternity inform us, that the ufages and cuftoms among mafons have ever correfponded with thofe of the ancient Egyptians, to which they bear a near affinity. Thefe philofophers, unwilling to expofe their myfteries to vulgar eyes, couched their particular tenets and principles of polity under hieroglyphical figures, and expreffed their notions of government by figns and fymbols, which they communicated to their Magi alone, and they were bound by oath not to reveal them. Hence arofe the

the Pythagorean fyftem, and many other orders of a more modern date. Mafonry, however, is not only the moft ancient, but the moft moral fociety that ever fubfifted; for every character, figure, and emblem, adopted by mafons, has a moral tendency, and ferves to inculcate the practice of virtue.

The Fifth Section.

The fifth fection informs us concerning the nature and principles of our conftitution, and teaches us to difcharge with propriety the duties of the different departments, which we are nominated to fuftain. Here too, our ornaments are difplayed, our jewels and furniture are fpecified, and our patrons are diftinguifhed.

To this remark we can add but little to explain the fubject of the fection, or to affift the induftrious mafon in attaining it. A punctual attendance on the duties of the fociety we would recommend as the moft effectual means to enable him to
gain

gain a knowledge of it; and a diligent application to the truths it demonstrates will certainly induce him to imitate the example of the original patrons of the Art.

The Sixth Section.

The sixth section, though the last in rank, is not the least considerable in importance. It strengthens these which precede, and enforces, in the most engaging manner, a due regard to our character and behaviour in public as well as private life; in our lodges, as well as in the commerce of society.

Of all the sections in this degree, the sixth particularly claims our attention. It not only retains many of the ancient landmarks of the Order, but forcibly inculcates the most instructive lessons. Brotherly love, relief, and truth, are the themes on which we here illustrate; and the cardinal virtues do not escape our notice. By the exercise of brotherly love we are

taught

taught to regard the whole human species as one family, the high and low, the rich and poor, created by one Almighty Being, and sent into the world for the aid, support, and protection of each other. On this principle, Masonry unites men of every country, sect, and opinion, and conciliates true friendship among persons who might otherwise have remained at a perpetual distance.—Relief is the next tenet of our profession. To relieve the distressed is a duty incumbent on all men, but particularly on masons, who are linked together by an indissoluble chain of sincere affection. To sooth the unhappy, to sympathize with their misfortunes, to compassionate their miseries, and to restore peace to their troubled minds, is the grand aim we have in view. On this basis we establish our friendships and form our connexions. —Truth is a divine attribute and the foundation of all masonic virtue. On this grand theme we contemplate, and by its dictates endeavour to regulate our conduct; hence hypocrisy and deceit are unknown

known to us, sincerity and plain dealing are our distinguishing characteristics, and the heart and tongue join in promoting each other's welfare, and in rejoicing in each other's prosperity.

When these principles are explained, our line of conduct is beautifully drawn in an illustration of temperance, fortitude, prudence, and justice.—By the first, we are instructed to govern our passions and to check our unruly desires. The health of the body, and the dignity of the species, are equally concerned in a faithful observance of this virtue.—By the second, we are taught to resist temptations, and to encounter dangers with spirit and resolution. This virtue is equally distant from rashness and cowardice, and whoever possesses it is seldom shaken, and never overthrown by the storms that surround him.—By the third, we learn to regulate our conduct by the dictates of reason, and to judge and determine with propriety in the execution of every thing that tends either to promote our present or future well being.

On this virtue all the others depend; it is therefore the chief jewel that can adorn the human frame.—Justice, though the last in rank, constitutes the cement of civil society. Without the exercise of this virtue, universal confusion would ensue. Lawless force would overcome the principles of equity, and social intercourse no longer exist. As justice in a great measure constitutes the real good man, so it is represented as the perpetual study of the accomplished mason.

Such is the mode of arrangement of the different sections in the first lecture, which, with the forms adopted at the opening and closing of our assemblies, comprehend the whole of the first degree of Masonry. This mode, while it is free from tautology, has the support of precedent and authority, and the sanction and respect which flow from antiquity. The whole is one regular system of morality, conceived in a strain of interesting allegory, which unfolds its beauties to the candid and industrious inquirer.

SECOND LECTURE.

Masonry includes within its circle almost every branch of polite literature. Under the sanction of its mysteries is comprehended a regular system of science. Many of its illustrations to the confined genius may probably appear dull, trifling, and unimportant; but to the man of more enlarged faculties they will appear in the highest degree useful and interesting. To please the accomplished scholar and the ingenious artist, Masonry is wisely planned; and, in the investigation of its latent doctrines, the sage philosopher will experience delight and satisfaction.

To exhaust the various subjects of which Masonry treats, would transcend the powers of the brightest genius; still, however, nearer approaches to perfection may be made, and the man of wisdom will never check the progress of his abilities, though the talk he attempts may seem arduous and infurmountable. Perfeverance and application will remove each difficulty as it occurs; every ftep he advances, new pleafures will open to his view, and inftruction of the nobleft kind attend his curious refearches. In the diligent purfuit of knowledge great difcoveries are made, and the intellectual faculties are employed in the grand defign of promoting the glory of God, and the good of man.

Such is the refult of all our illuftrations in Mafonry. To promote fcience, reward induftry, and encourage ingenuity, is the general fcope of all our meafures. Reverence for the Deity, and gratitude for the bleffings of heaven, are inculcated in every degree. This is the termination of our inquiries, and beyond this the bounds of our capacity cannot reach.

The firft degree is well calculated to enforce the duties of morality, and imprint on the memory the nobleft principles which can adorn the human mind. It is therefore

therefore the best introduction to the second degree, which not only extends the same plan, but comprehends a more diffusive system of knowledge. Practice and theory join in qualifying the industrious mason to share the pleasures which an advancement in the Art must necessarily afford him. Listening with attention to the wise opinions of experienced craftsmen on important subjects, he gradually familiarizes his mind to useful instruction, and is soon enabled to investigate truths of the utmost concern in the general transactions of life.

From this system of knowledge proceeds a rational amusement; while the mental powers are fully exercised, the dignity of human nature is properly supported. Thus a spirit of emulation universally prevails, and we are naturally induced to vie in promoting the excellent rules of our venerable institution.

The First Section.

The first section of the second degree of Masonry elucidates with accuracy the mode of introduction into this particular clafs, and inftructs the diligent craftfman how to proceed with regularity in the proper arrangement of the ceremonies ufed on the occafion. It qualifies him to judge of the importance of thefe ceremonies, and convinces him of the neceffity of ftrictly adhering to every eftablifhed ufage in the fociety. Here he is entrufted with the knowledge of particular tefts, to enable him to prove his title to the privileges of this degree, and fatisfactory reafons are given for their origin. Many duties which cement in the firmeft union our well-informed brethren, are illuftrated in this fection; and an opportunity is here given to make farther advances in Mafonry, and to diftinguifh the abilities of all perfons who have arrived at this honourable preferment.

The knowledge of this fection is abfolutely neceffary for every mafon who has advanced to this degree. It not only recapitulates the ceremony of initiation, but contains many particulars, of which our

ignorance

ignorance may expose us to derision. The following charge will remind the craftsman of his duty.

Charge at Initiation into the Second Degree *.

BROTHER,

Being now advanced to the second degree of Masonry, it is necessary to congratulate you on your preferment. [You must know, that the internal, and not the external, qualifications of a man, are what Masonry regards. As you increase in knowledge, you will consequently improve in social intercourse.

It is unnecessary to recapitulate the several duties, which, as a mason, you are bound to discharge; or enlarge on the necessity of a strict adherence to them, as your own experience must have convinced you of their importance and utility. It may be sufficient to observe, that] Your past behaviour and regular deportment has me-

* The sentences inclosed in brackets [ ] may be occasionally omitted.

rited

rited the additional honour which we now confer; and in your new character, it is expected you will always conform to the principles of Masonry, and steadily persevere in the practice of every commendable virtue.

The study of the liberal arts, [that valuable branch of education, which tends so effectually to polish and adorn the human mind,] is earnestly recommended to your serious consideration; especially the science of geometry, which is established as the basis of our Art. [Masonry being both of a divine and moral nature, is enriched with the most useful knowledge; while it proves the wonderful properties of nature, it also demonstrates the more important truths of morality.]

As the solemnity of our different ceremonies requires a grave and serious deportment, you are to be particularly attentive to your behaviour in our regular assemblies; to preserve the ancient usages and customs of the fraternity sacred and inviolable; and endeavour to induce others,

others, by your example, to hold them in due veneration.

The laws and regulations of the society you are to support and maintain; and be ever ready to assist in seeing them duly executed. You are not to palliate or aggravate the offences of your brethren; but, in the decision of every trespass against our rules, you are to judge with candour, to admonish with friendship, and to reprehend with justice.

In our private assemblies, you are to offer your sentiments and opinions on various subjects, so far as they correspond with, and are agreeable to, the tenets of Masonry. Thus you will improve your rational and intellectual powers; qualify yourself to become an useful member of society; and vie with your brethren, in your endeavours to excell in every thing that is good and great.

* Every regular sign or summons, given and received, you are duly to honour, and

---

* This and the following paragraph are to be omitted, if previously used in the course of the ceremony.

punctually to obey; infomuch as they confift with our profeffed principles. You are cheerfully to relieve the neceffities of your brethren to the utmoft of your power and ability, without prejudice to yourfelf or your private concerns : and you are, on no account, to injure a brother, or to fee him injured; but you are to apprife him of all approaching dangers, and view his intereft as your own.

Such is the nature of your prefent engagements; and to thefe duties you are now bound by the moft facred ties.

The Second Section.

The fecond fection of this degree prefents to view an ample field for the man of genius to perambulate. While it curforily fpecifies the particular claffes of Mafonry, it explains the requifite qualifications for preferment in each. In the explanation of our ufages many remarks are introduced, equally ufeful to the experienced artift and the fage moralift. The various operations of the human
mind

mind are demonstrated as far as they will admit of elucidation, and a fund of extensive science is explored throughout. Here we find employment for leisure hours, trace science from its original source, and contemplate with admiration the wonderful works of the Creator. Geometry is displayed with all its powers and properties; and, in the curious disquisition of this valuable science, the mathematician and philosopher may experience equal delight. Such is the latitude of this section, that the most judicious may fail in their attempts to explain it, as the rational powers are exerted to their utmost stretch, in illustrating the beauties of nature, and demonstrating the more important truths of morality.

As the orders of architecture come under our consideration in the disquisition of this section, a brief description of them may be here necessary.

By order in architecture is meant a system of all the ornaments and propor tions of columns and pilasters, or a regular arrangement of all the projecting parts of a building, more especially those of a column, which form one beautiful, perfect, and complete whole. From the first formation of human society they date their origin. When the rigour of the seasons obliged men to contrive huts to shelter themselves from the inclemency of the weather, they planted trees on end, and then laid others across to support a covering. The bands which connected these trees at top and bottom are said to have given rise to the idea of the base and capital of pillars, and from this simple hint originally proceeded the art of architecture.

The five principal orders are, the Tuscan, Doric, Ionic, Corinthian, and Composite.

The Tuscan is the most simple and solid of the five orders. It was invented in Tuscany, from whence it derives its name. Its column is seven diameters high, and its capital, base, and entablature

ture have but few mouldings or ornaments, yet there is a peculiar beauty in its simplicity which adds to its value, and makes it fit to be used in structures where the more rich and delicate orders would be improper.

The Doric order is the most agreeable to nature. It is the most ancient, and was first invented by the Greeks. Its column is eight diameters high, and it has no ornament either on base or capital. Its frieze is distinguished by triglyphs and metopes, and the triglyphs compose the ornaments of the frieze. The composition of this order is both grand and noble, and it is therefore used principally in warlike structures, where strength, and a noble, but rough simplicity, are required.

The Ionic order bears a kind of mean proportion between the more solid and delicate orders. Its column is nine diameters high, its capital is adorned with volutes, and its cornice has denticles. History informs us, that the famous temple of Diana at Ephesus was of this order.

The Corinthian is the richest of the five orders. It is deemed a master-piece of art, and was invented at Corinth by Callimachus. Its column is ten diameters high, and its capital is adorned with two rows of leaves, and eight volutes which sustain the abacus. This order is generally used in stately and superb structures.

The Composite or Roman order is derived from the other orders. Its capital has the two rows of leaves of the Corinthian, and the volutes of the Ionic. Its column has the quarter-round as the Tuscan and Doric orders, is ten diameters high, and its cornice has denticles or simple modillions. To the Romans we are indebted for the invention of this pillar, which is generally found in buildings where strength, elegance, and beauty are displayed.

In an analysis of the human faculties, which is given in the course of this section, the five external senses claim our attention.

attention. We shall therefore annex a brief description of them*.

Hearing is that sense by which we are enabled to distinguish sounds, and are made capable of the perceptions of harmony and melody, with all the agreeable charms of music. By it we are enabled to enjoy the pleasures of society, and reciprocally to communicate to each other our thoughts and intentions, our purposes and desires; and by means of this sense our reason is capable of exerting its utmost power and energy.

Seeing is that sense by which we are enabled to distinguish objects of different kinds, and in an instant of time, without change of place or situation; to view whole armies in battle array, figures of the most stately structures, and all the agreeable variety displayed in the landscape of nature. By it we can find our way in the pathless ocean, traverse the globe of earth, determine its figure and dimensions, and delineate any region or

* See Dr. Reid's Inquiry into the Human Mind.

quarter of it. By it we can measure the planetary orbs, and make new discoveries in the sphere of the fixed stars. Nay more, by this sense we can perceive the tempers and dispositions, the passions and affections of our fellow-creatures, when they wish most to conceal them; so that though the tongue be taught to lie and dissemble, the countenance will display the hypocrisy to the discerning eye. In fine, the rays of light which administer to this sense are the most astonishing parts of the inanimate creation, and render the eye, with all its appurtenances, the masterpiece of Nature's work.

Feeling is that sense by which we are enabled to distinguish the different qualities of bodies, and those of different kinds; such as heat and cold, hardness and softness, roughness and smoothness, figure, solidity, motion, and extension; all of which, by means of certain corresponding sensations of touch, are presented to the mind as real external qualities, and the conception or belief of them invariably connected with these corresponding sensations by an original principle

ciple of human nature, which far tranfcends our inquiry.

Smelling is that fenfe by which we are enabled to diftinguifh odours of various kinds, each of which has a different impreffion on the mind. Animal and vegetable bodies, and indeed moft other bodies, while expofed to the air, are continually fending forth effluvia of vaft fubtilty, not only in their ftate of life and growth, but in the ftates of fermentation and putrefaction. Thefe volatile particles probably repel each other, and fcatter themfelves in the air, till they unite with other bodies to which they bear fome chymical affinity, with which they unite, and form new concretes. Thefe effluvia are drawn into the noftrils along with the air, and are the means by which all bodies are fmelled. So that there is a manifeft appearance of defign in the great Creator's having planted the organ of fmell in the infide of that canal, through which the air continually paffes, as well in infpiration as in expiration.

Tafting enables us to make a proper diftinction in the choice of our food.

The

The organ of this sense guards the entrance of the alimentary canal, as that of smell the entrance of the canal for respiration. From the situation of these organs, it is plain that they were intended by Nature to distinguish wholesome food from that which is noxious. Every thing that enters into the stomach must undergo the scrutiny of Tasting; and by it we are capable of discerning all the changes which the same body undergoes in the different compositions of art.

For an illustration of the advantages resulting from Geometry in an expanded sense, on which we are likewise led to expatiate in this section, we must refer back to the Vindication of Masonry, p. 13.

The Third Section.

The third section of this degree has recourse to the origin of the institution, and views Masonry under two denominations, operative and speculative. Each is separately considered, and the principles on which both are founded, are particularly explained.

explained. Their affinity is pointed out, and their connexion demonstrated by allegorical figures and typical representations. Here the rise of our government, or division into classes, is examined; the disposition of our rulers, supreme and subordinate, is traced; and reasons are assigned for the establishment of several of our present practices. The progress made in architecture, particularly in the reign of Solomon, is here remarked; the number of artists employed in building the temple of Jerusalem, with their privileges, are specified; and many other particulars are here recited, all of which have been carefully preserved among masons, and communicated from one age to another by oral tradition. The marks of distinction, conferred on our ancient brethren as the reward of excellence, are here named; and the duties, as well as the privileges, of their male offspring, carefully enumerated. In short, this section contains a store of useful knowledge, founded on reason and sacred record, both entertaining and instructive. The whole operates

powerfully

powerfully in enforcing the respect and veneration due to antiquity.

We can afford no assistance to the industrious mason in this section; it can only be acquired by verbal instruction. For an explanation of the connexion betwixt operative and speculative Masonry, however, we would recommend him to peruse the sixth section of the Vindication, p. 17.

The Fourth Section.

The fourth and last section of this degree is no less replete with wise and useful instruction. Circumstances of great importance to the society are here particularised, and many of our traditional tenets and customs confirmed by sacred and profane history. The celestial and terrestrial globes are considered with a minute accuracy, and the accomplished gentleman may here display his talents to great advantage, in the elucidation of the sciences, which are classed in a regular arrangement.

ment. This section contains observations on the validity of some of our forms, and concludes with the most powerful incentives to piety and virtue.

As the seven liberal arts and sciences are illustrated in this section, it may not be improper to insert here a short explanation of them.

Grammar teaches us the proper arrangement of words according to the idiom or dialect of any particular kingdom or people; and that excellency of pronunciation, which enables us to speak or write a language with accuracy and justness, agreeable to reason, authority, and the strict rules of literature.

Rhetoric teaches us to speak copiously and fluently on any subject, not merely with propriety alone, but with all the advantages of force, elegance, and beauty, wisely contriving to captivate the hearer by strength of argument and beauty of expression, whether it be to entreat and exhort, to admonish or applaud.

Logic teaches us to guide our reason discretionally in the general knowledge of things, and to direct our inquiries after truth, as well for the instruction of others as our own improvement. It consists of a regular train of argument, whence we infer, deduce, and conclude, according to certain premises laid down, admitted, or granted. In it are employed the faculties of conceiving, judging, reasoning, and disposing; all of which are naturally led on from one gradation to another, till the point in question is finally determined.

Arithmetic teaches us to deduce the powers and properties of numbers, which is variously effected by letters, tables, figures, and instruments. By this art, reasons and demonstrations are given for finding out any certain number, whose relation or affinity to another number is already known or discovered.

Geometry treats of the powers and properties of magnitudes in general, where length, length and breadth, or length, breadth

breadth and thickness are considered. By this science the architect is enabled to estimate his plans and execute his designs; the general to arrange his soldiers; the engineer to mark out ground for encampments; the geographer to give us the dimensions of the world, and all things therein contained, to delineate the extent of seas, and specify the divisions of empires, kingdoms, and provinces; and by it the astronomer is also enabled to make his observations, and to fix the duration of times and seasons, years and cycles. In fine, geometry is the foundation of architecture, and the root of the mathematics.

Music teaches us the art of forming concords so as to make delightful harmony by a mathematical and proportional arrangement of acute, grave, and mixed sounds. This art is by a series of experiments reduced to a demonstrative science with respect to tones and the intervals of sound only. It inquires into the nature of concords and discords, and enables us to find out the proportion between them by numbers.

Astronomy,

Aſtronomy, though the laſt, is not the leaſt important ſcience. It is that divine art by which we are taught to read the wiſdom, ſtrength, and beauty of the almighty Creator in thoſe ſacred pages, the celeſtial hemiſphere. Aſſiſted by aſtronomy, we can obſerve the motions, meaſure the diſtances, comprehend the magnitudes, and calculate the periods and eclipſes of the heavenly bodies. By it we learn the uſe of the globes, the ſyſtem of the world, and the primary law of nature. While we are employed in the ſtudy of this ſcience, we perceive unparalleled inſtances of wiſdom and goodneſs, and on every hand may trace the glorious Author by his works.

As the doctrine of the ſpheres is included in the ſcience of aſtronomy, and particularly conſidered in this ſection, we ſhall here inſert a brief deſcription of theſe bodies.

The globes are two artificial ſpherical bodies, on the convex ſurface of which are repreſented the countries, ſeas, and various parts of the earth, the face of the heavens, the planetary revolutions, and several other particulars of equal importance. The sphere with the parts of the earth delineated on its surface, is called the terrestrial globe; and that with the constellations and other heavenly bodies, the celestial globe. Their principal use, beside serving as maps to distinguish the outward parts of the earth, and the situation of the fixed stars, is to illustrate and explain the phænomena arising from the annual motion of the sun, and the diurnal rotation of the earth round its own axis. They are the noblest instruments for improving the mind, and giving it the most clear and distinct ideas of any problem or proposition, as well as enabling it to solve the same. By employing ourselves in the knowledge of these bodies, we are not only inspired with a due reverence for the Deity, but are also induced to apply with more anxiety and attention to the sciences of astronomy, geography, navigation, &c.

Thus end the different sections of the second lecture, which, with the ceremonies used at opening and closing the lodge, comprehend the whole of the second degree of Masonry. This lecture contains a regular system of science, demonstrated on the clearest principles, and founded on the most stable foundation. By these means our diligent craftsmen are distinguished, and hence they are induced to excel in every thing that is good and great.

THIRD LECTURE.

In treating with propriety on any subject, it is necessary to observe a regular course. In the two first degrees of Masonry, I have recapitulated the contents of the several sections, and would willingly pursue the same measures in the third degree, did not the variety of particulars contained in it, render it impossible to give an abstract of them, without violating the laws of the Order. I shall only remark, that in twelve sections, of which

this

this lecture confists, every circumstance is accurately explained, which relates either to our government, or the mode of our proceedings on private or public occasions. Here the ancient landmarks of the society are preserved, and the expert and ingenious craftsman is qualified to discharge every duty in the craft with honour and reputation. To the knowledge of this degree few indeed arrive, but it is an infallible truth, that he who merits the privileges of a master-mason, here meets with his just reward; a reward which amply compensates for all his past labour and assiduity. By employing his abilities in the pursuit of useful knowledge, he demonstrates his wisdom, and is justly entitled to respect and veneration.

From this class our rulers must be selected; as it is from those who are capable of giving instruction, we can only expect to receive it.

The First Section.

The first section serves as an introduction to the third degree, and contains many particulars to diftinguifh the moft deferving craftfmen, and prove their title to the privileges of the refpectable order of mafter-mafons.

In this fection we are inftructed in the ceremony of opening a Chapter of the Order, and the matter of which it confifts recalls to our memory the moft important circumftances of the preceding degrees.

The Second Section.

The ceremony of initiation into the third degree is particularly fpecified in the fecond fection, and in it many ufeful inftructions are given.

Of fuch general utility and importance is the knowledge of this fection, that we may fafely declare that no mafon can be qualified in any meafure to accept an office in the fociety, as a ruler or governor of the work, who is unacquainted with it.

Prayer at Initiation into the Third Degree.

O Lord, direct us, thy faithful servants, to know and serve thee aright, prosper all our laudable undertakings, and grant that, as we increase in knowledge, we may improve in piety and virtue, and still further promote thy honour and glory. Amen.

Charge at Initiation into the Third Degree.

BROTHER,

Your zeal for this honourable institution, your knowledge in our sacred mysteries, and your stedfast conformity to all our wise and useful regulations, have pointed you out as a proper object for this distinguishing mark of our fraternal affection.

Duty, honour, and gratitude, now bind you to be faithful to every trust; to support the dignity of Masonry on all occasions, and to recommend a due obedience to its excellent tenets. To the duties contained in our various lectures you are
strictly

strictly to adhere, and by precept and example enforce our laws: Thus the world will be convinced that merit is the only title to our privileges, and that on you our favours are not undeservedly bestowed.

In the character of a master-mason, you are authorized to correct the irregularities of your brethren; if any of them have, through heedlessness and inattention, deviated from our excellent rules. You are to be to them a perpetual monitor of their errors, to fortify their minds with resolution to resist the temptations of the wild and imprudent, and to guard them against every allurement to vicious practices. On all occasions you are to caution the inexperienced against a breach of fidelity; and, as much as lies in your power, preserve the reputation of the society at large. You are to recommend to your inferiors, obedience and submission; to your equals, courtesy and affability; and to your superiors, kindness and condescension. Universal benevolence you are zealously to inculcate;

inculcate; and qualify yourself, by argument, to remove every aspersion against this venerable institution. Our ancient landmarks you are carefully to preserve, and never to suffer an infringement of them; or, on any pretence, to countenance deviations from our established usages and customs.

Your virtue, your honour, your reputation, are all equally concerned in supporting, with becoming dignity, the character in which you now appear. Let no motive therefore make you swerve from your duty, violate your vows, or betray your trust; but be true and faithful, and imitate the example of that celebrated artist, whom you have this evening represented. Thus you will prove yourself worthy of the confidence that we have reposed in you, and deserving of every honour which we can confer.

The Third Section.

The third section serves as a preliminary introduction to the historical traditions of the Order, collected from sacred record, and other authentic writings.

The Fourth Section.

The fourth section consists of historical traditions concerning the Order, of the utmost consequence to the fraternity.

The Fifth Section.

In the fifth section, the historical traditions of the Order are continued.

The Sixth Section.

In the sixth section, the historical traditions of the Order are concluded.

The Seventh Section.

In the seventh section, many useful lessons are inculcated, for the extending of knowledge and promoting of virtue.

The Eighth Section.

The eighth section considers the government of the society, and the disposition of its rulers.

The Ninth Section.

The ninth section illustrates the qualifications of our rulers, and includes the mode of installation, both in the grand lodge and private lodges*.

The Tenth Section.

The tenth section comprehends the ceremonies of constitution and consecration, with many particulars explanatory of them.

The Eleventh Section.

The eleventh section consists of the forms and ceremonies used on public occasions; as, at funerals; laying the foundation stones of churches, chapels, hospitals, &c.

The Twelfth Section.

The twelfth section considers the most remarkable circumstances in the various

---

* For a particular account of many circumstances to which this and the two following sections relate, see the Ceremonies of Constitution, Consecration, Installation, &c. annexed to these Remarks.

degrees of Masonry, and corroborates the whole by the most infallible testimony.

Having thus gone through the principal degrees of Masonry, and made such remarks on the several sections of each, as I conceived would illustrate the subject of them, I am in hopes the zealous mason will be encouraged to persevere in his researches. When he has advanced to the conclusion of the third degree, he will find himself qualified to support, with propriety, in his own character, every office in the society; and he will certainly merit the esteem and approbation of all good men, for having employed his leisure hours in the cultivation and improvement of a science, both useful and interesting.

I shall now proceed to illustrate the ceremonies observed at the constitution and consecration of a lodge, with the mode of installation of officers; and introduce the charges usually delivered on
those

those occasions in their proper places. To these remarks I will likewise annex an explanation of the ceremonies used at laying the foundation stones of public structures, and at funerals, and will close this part of my treatise with the service rehearsed previous to, and at the time of interment.

The Manner of constituting a Lodge, according to ancient Usage: with the Ceremony of Consecration, &c.

ANY number of Master-masons, not under seven, resolved to form themselves into a New Lodge, must apply, by petition, to the Grand Master; setting forth,
'That they are regular-made masons, and
'present members of different lodges un-
'der the constitution of England: ‚That
'they have the prosperity of the society
'at heart, and are willing to exert their
'best endeavours to promote the prin-
'ciples of Masonry: That, for the con-
'veniency of their respective dwellings,
'and other good reasons, they have agreed

'to form themselves into a New Lodge,
'to be named   , and have nomi-
'nated A. B. to be the Master, C. D.
'to be the Senior Warden, and E. F.
'to be the Junior Warden: That, in
'consequence of this resolution, they pray
'for a warrant of constitution, to em-
'power them to assemble, and hold a
'regular lodge on the   of every
'month, at
'and then and there to make, pass, and
'raise masons, according to the regular
'forms of the society, and to execute all
'the other duties of the craft: That, the
'prayer of their petition being granted,
'they will faithfully obey all the edicts
'or commands of the Grand Master, and
'strictly conform to all the laws and re-
'gulations of the Grand Lodge.'

This petition, being properly signed, and recommended by three Masters of regular lodges, nearest adjacent to the place where the new lodge is proposed to be held, must be delivered to the Grand Secretary; who, on presenting it to the Deputy

Deputy Grand Master, and his approving of it, will grant a dispensation; authorising the brethren specified in it, to assemble as masons for forty days, or until such time as a constitution shall be granted, or that authority be recalled.

In consequence of this dispensation, a lodge may be held at the place there specified; and its transactions, being properly recorded, will be equally valid, for the time being, with those of a regular constituted lodge.

The petition is presented by the Deputy Grand Master to the Grand Master, who being satisfied of the truth of the allegations it contains, appoints a day and hour for constituting [and consecrating*] this New Lodge; and for installing the Master, Wardens, and other officers of the same.

If the Grand Master attends, with all his Officers, the lodge will be constituted IN AMPLE FORM; if the Deputy Grand Master and the other Grand Officers attend,

* This is too frequently omitted.

tend, it will be constituted IN DUE FORM; but if the power is vested in any subordinate lodge, it will only be constituted IN FORM.

On the day and hour appointed, the Grand Master, with his Officers, [or the Master and Officers of any private lodge authorized by the Grand Master,] meet in a convenient room, and being properly clothed, walk in procession to the lodge room. The lodge is opened by the Grand Master in all the degrees of Masonry. A prayer being repeated in due form, and an ode in honour of the society sung, the Grand Master [or Master in the Chair] is informed, 'That a certain number of
' brethren then present, duly instructed
' in the mysteries of Masonry, desire to
' be formed into a New Lodge, under
' his Worship's [or the Grand Master's]
' patronage; that a dispensation had been
' granted to them, by virtue of which
' authority they had assembled as regular
' masons; and that the transactions of
' their several meetings had been properly
' recorded.'

'recorded.' The petition is then read, as is also the dispensation, and the warrant or charter of constitution, granted in consequence of it. The minutes of all the transactions of the New Lodge, while under dispensation, are likewise read, and being approved, they are declared to be regular and valid. Then the Grand Master [or Master in the Chair] takes the warrant in his hand, and requests the brethren of the New Lodge, to signify their approbation or disapprobation of the officers nominated in the said warrant to preside over them. This being signified accordingly, an anthem is sung, and an oration on the nature and design of Masonry is delivered.

Ceremony of Consecration*.

The Grand Master, attended by his Officers, and some dignified Clergyman, form themselves in order round the lodge in the center. All devoutly kneeling,

* This is never to be used but when specially ordered.

the

the preparatory prayer is rehearsed. The chaplain produces his authority, and being properly assisted, proceeds to consecrate. Solemn music strikes up, and the necessary preparations are made. The first clause of the consecration prayer is rehearsed, all devoutly kneeling. The response is made, GLORY TO GOD ON HIGH. Incense is scattered over the lodge, and the grand honours of Masonry are given. The consecration prayer is concluded, and the response repeated, together with the grand honours, as before. All rising up, solemn music is introduced, after which the blessing is given, and the response made as before, accompanied with the usual honours. An anthem is then sung, and the brethren of the New Lodge coming forward and doing homage, the Grand Master pronounces these words:

' In this my exalted character, and in
' the name of the MOST HIGH, to whom
' be glory and honour, I constitute and
' form these good brethren into a regu-
' lar

' lar Lodge of Free and Accepted Ma-
' fons; and God be with them.' Amen.
[Flourish with drums and trumpets.]

The grand honours are once more repeated, and the ceremony of confecration ends.

Ceremony of Inftallation.

The Grand Mafter * then afks his deputy, ' If he has examined the mafter
' nominated in the warrant, and whether
' he finds him well fkilled in the noble
' fcience and the royal Art?' The deputy anfwering in the affirmative, he, by the Grand Mafter's order, takes the candidate from among his fellows, and prefents him at the pedeftal; faying, ' Moft
' worshipful Grand Mafter, [or right wor-
' shipful, as it happens,] I prefent my
' worthy brother A. B. to be inftalled
' Mafter of this New Lodge. I know
' him to be of good morals and of great

* In this, and other fimilar inftances, where the Grand Mafter is fpecified as acting, may be underftood any Mafter who performs the ceremony.

' fkill,

' skill, true and trusty, and a lover of the
' whole fraternity, wheresoever dispersed
' over the face of the earth.'

The following charges † are then read by the Grand secretary [or acting Secretary] to the Master Elect.

' I. You

---

† As it may be agreeable to the curious reader to know the ancient charges that were used on this occasion, we shall here insert them *verbatim*, as they are contained in a MS. in the possession of the Lodge of Antiquity, written in the reign of James the Second.

' * * * * * And furthermore, at diverse assem-
' blies have been put and ordained diverse crafties
' by the best advise of magistrates and fellows.
' *Tunc unus ex senioribus tent. librum, et illi ponent ma-*
' *num suam super librum.*

  ' Every man that is a mason take good heed to
' these charges (wee pray) that if any man find him-
' selfe guilty of any of these charges, that he may
' amend himselfe, or principally for dread of God,
' you that be charged to take good heed that you
' keepe all these charges well, for it is a great evill
' for a man to forswear himselfe upon a book.

  ' The first charge is, That yee shall be true men
' to God and the holy church, and to use no error
' or heresie by your understanding and by wise men's
' teaching. Allso,

' Secondly,

' I. You are to be a good man and true,
' and strictly to obey the moral law.

' II. You

' Secondly, That yee shall be true liege men to
' the King of England, without treason or any fals-
' hood, and that yee know no treason or treachery,
' but yee shall give knowledge thereof to the King,
' or to his counsell; allso yee shall be true one to
' another, (that is to say) every mason of the craft
' that is mason allowed, yee shall doe to him as yee
' would be done unto yourselfe.

' Thirdly, And yee shall keepe truly all the
' counsell that ought to be kept in the way of Ma-
' sonhood, and all the counsell of the Lodge or of
' the chamber.—Allso, that yee shall be no theife
' nor theives to your knowledge free; that you shall
' be true to the king, lord, or master that yee serve,
' and truely to see and worke for his advantage.

' Fourthly, Yee shall call all masons your fel-
' lows, or your brethren, and no other names.

' Fifthly, Yee shall not take your fellow's wife
' in villany, nor deflower his daughter or servant,
' nor put him to no disworship.

' Sixthly, Yee shall truely pay for your meat or
' drinke wheresoever yee goe, to table or bord. Allso,
' yee shall doe no villany there, whereby the craft or
' science may be slandered.

' These be the charges general to every true ma-
' son, both masters and fellowes.

' Now will I rehearse other charges single for ma-
' sons allowed or accepted.

' First,

' II. You are to be a peaceable subject,
' and cheerfully to conform to the laws of
' the country in which you reside.

' III. You

' First, That no mason take on him no lord's
' worke, nor other man's, unlesse he know him-
' selfe well able to perform the worke, so that the
' craft have no slander.

' Secondly, Allso, that no master take worke
' but that he take reasonable pay for itt; so that
' the lord may be truely served, and the master to
' live honestly, and to pay his fellows truely. And
' that no master or fellow supplant others of their
' worke; (that is to say) that if he hath taken a
' worke, or else stand master of any worke, that he
' shall not put him out, unlefs he be unable of cun-
' ning to make an end of his worke. And no mas-
' ter nor fellow shall take no apprintice for lefs than
' seaven yeares. And that the apprintice be free-
' born, and of limbs whole as a man ought to be,
' and no bastard. And that no master or fellow take
' no allowance to be made mason without the assent
' of his fellows, at the least six or seaven.

' Thirdly, That he that be made be able in all
' degrees; that is, free-born, of a good kindred,
' true, and no bondsman, and that he have his right
' limbs as a man ought to have.

' Fourthly, that a master take no apprintice with-
' out he have occupation to occupie two or three
' fellows at the least.

' Fifthly,

'III. You are not to be concerned in
'plots or conspiracies against government,
'but submit to the decisions of legislative
'power.

'IV. You

'Fifthly, That no master or fellow put away any
'lord's worke to taske that ought to be journey
'worke.

'Sixthly, That every master give pay to his fel-
'lows and servants as they may deserve, soe that he
'be not defamed with false workeing. And that
'none slander another behind his backe, to make
'him loose his good name.

'Seaventhly, That no fellow in the house or
'abroad answear another ungodly or reproveablely
'without a cause.

'Eighthly, That every master-mason doe reve-
'rence his elder; and that a mason be no common
'plaier at the cards, dice, or hazzard, nor at other
'unlawfull plaies, through the which the science
'and craft may be dishonored or slandered.

'Ninthly, That no fellow goe into the town by
'night, except he have a fellow with him, who
'may beare him record that he was in an honest
'place.

'Tenthly, That every master and fellow shall
'come to the assemblie, if itt be within fifty miles
'of him, if he have any warning. And if he have
'trespassed against the craft, to abide the award of
'masters and fellows.

'Eleventhly,

'IV. You are to respect the civil magistrate, to work diligently, live creditably, and act honourably by all men.

'Eleventhly, That every master-mason and fellow that hath trespassed against the craft shall stand to the correction of other masters and fellows to make him accord, and if they cannot accord, to go to the common law.

'Twelvethly, That a master or fellow make not a mould-stone, square, nor rule to no lowen, nor let no lowen worke within their Lodge nor without to mould stone.

'Thirteenthly, That every mason receive and cherish strange fellowes, when they come over the countrie, and set them on worke if they will worke, as the manner is, (that is to say) if the mason have any mould stone in his place he shall give him a mould stone, and sett him on worke; and if he have none, the mason shall refresh him with money unto the next lodge.

'Fourteenthly, That every mason shall truely serve his master for his pay.

'Fifteenthly, That every master shall truely make an end of his worke, taske, or journey, whethersoe it be.

'These be all the charges and covenants that ought to be read at the installment of master, or makeing of a free-mason or free-masons. The almighty God of Jacob who ever have you and me in his keepeing, bless us now and ever. Amen.'

'V. You

'V. You are to obey the rulers and go-
'vernors of the fociety, fupreme and fub-
'ordinate, in their different ftations, and
'fubmit to the awards and refolutions of
'your brethren.

'VI. You are to avoid private piques
'and quarrels, and guard againft intem-
'perance and excefs.

'VII. You are to be cautious and pru-
'dent in your behaviour, courteous to
'your brethren, and faithful to the lodge
'to which you belong.

'VIII. You are to refpect your ge-
'nuine brethren, and difcountenance all
'falfe pretenders.

'IX. You are to promote the general
'good of fociety, cultivate the focial vir-
'tues, and be always ready to give or to
'receive inftruction.'

The Secretary then reads the following regulations.

'I. The Grand Mafter for the time be-
'ing, and all his officers are to be duly
'homaged, and the edicts of the Grand
'Lodge be ftrictly enforced.

'II. No alteration or innovation in the
'body of Masonry shall be made without
'the consent of the Grand Lodge first had
'and obtained.

'III. The duties of the Grand Lodge
'are to be regularly attended, and the
'dignity of the society supported.

'IV. No stated Lodge is to be formed
'without leave from the Grand Master or
'his Deputy, or any countenance given
'to a mason clandestinely made in such
'Lodge.

'V. No mason is to be made, or mem-
'ber admitted, in a regular Lodge, with-
'out one month's previous notice, or due
'inquiry into his character.

'VI. No visitors are to be received into
'a Lodge unless vouchers can be pro-
'duced of their having been initiated in
'a regular constituted Lodge, acting un-
'der the authority of the Grand Master
'of England, or some other Grand Master
'approved by him.

'VII. No public processions of masons
'clothed with the badges of the Order, are
'to

' to be countenanced without the special
' licence of the Grand Master.

' These are the laws and regulations of
' the society of Free and Accepted Masons.

The Grand Master then addresses the Master elect in the following manner: ' Do you submit to these charges, and ' do you promise to support these regu- ' lations, as Masters have done in all ' ages?' The New Master having signified his cordial submission, is bound to his trust, and invested with the badge of his office by the Grand Master, who thus salutes him: ' Brother A. B. in conse- ' quence of the recommendation I have ' received of you, and your cheerful con- ' formity to the charges and regulations ' of the society, I appoint you Master of ' this New Lodge, not doubting of your ' care, skill, and capacity.' The warrant of constitution is then delivered over to the New Master; after which the Holy Bible, the square and compass, the book of constitutions, the minute book, the hiram, the moveable

moveable jewels, and all the infignia of his different officers, are feparately prefented to him, and the neceffary charges fuitable to each, are properly delivered*. The New Mafter is then conducted by the Stewards, amidft the acclamations of the brethren, to the Grand Mafter's left hand, where he returns his becoming acknowledgments; to the Grand Mafter firft, and to all the reft in their order: after which he is faluted by the mufic, with a fong fuitable to the occafion. The members of the New Lodge next advance, pay due homage to the Grand Mafter, and fignify their promife of fubjection and obedience to their New Mafter, by the ufual congratulations in the different degrees of Mafonry.

The Grand Mafter orders the New Mafter to enter immediately upon the exercife of his office; to wit, in appointing his wardens, whom he accordingly names. They are conducted up to

* The fame ceremony and charges attend every fucceeding inftallation.

the

the pedeſtal, and preſented to the Grand Maſter; after which the New Maſter proceeds to inveſt them with the badges of their offices in the following manner:

‘ Brother C. D. I appoint you Senior
‘ Warden of this Lodge; and inveſt you
‘ with the enſign of your office *. Your
‘ regular and early attendance I particu-
‘ larly requeſt; as in my abſence you are
‘ to govern the lodge, and in my pre-
‘ ſence to aſſiſt me in the government of
‘ it. Your attachment to this lodge,
‘ joined to your knowledge of Maſonry,
‘ will, no doubt, enable you to diſcharge
‘ the duties of this important ſtation with
‘ honour and reputation.’

‘ Brother E. F. I appoint you Junior
‘ Warden of this lodge; and inveſt you
‘ with the badge of your office *. To
‘ you I entruſt the examination of viſitors,
‘ and the introduction of candidates. I
‘ therefore requeſt your regular and punc-
‘ tual attendance on the lodge. Your

* Here ſpecify its moral excellence.

‘ proficiency

'proficiency in Masonry, I doubt not,
'will qualify you to execute faithfully the
'duty you owe to your present appoint-
'ment.'

'Brother Wardens, you are both too
'good members of our community, and
'too expert in the principles of Masonry,
'to require much information in the du-
'ties of your respective offices: suffice
'it to mention, that I expect what you
'have seen praise-worthy in others, you
'will carefully imitate; and what in them
'may have appeared defective, you will
'carefully avoid. Good order and regu-
'larity you must endeavour to promote.
'By a due regard to the laws in your
'own conduct, you can only expect to
'enforce a due obedience to them in that
'of the other members.'

The Wardens retire to their seats, and the Treasurer * is next invested. The Secretary is then called up to the pedestal, and invested with the jewel of his office;

* This officer is not appointed by the Master, but elected by the lodge.

upon

upon which the New Master thus addresses him:

'I appoint you, brother G. H., Secretary of this lodge. It is your province to record the minutes, settle the accounts, and issue out the summons for our regular meetings. Your good inclinations to Masonry will certainly induce you to discharge this trust with fidelity, and in so doing you will justly merit the esteem and applause of the lodge.'

The Stewards are next called up and invested, and the following charge is delivered by the New Master:

'Brother I. K. and brother L. M. I appoint you Stewards of the lodge. The duties of your office are to introduce visitors, and to see that they are properly accommodated; to collect the quarterage and other fees, and to keep an account of the lodge expences. Your regular and early attendance will be the best proof you can give of your zeal for Masonry, and your attachment to this lodge.'

The Master then appoints the Tyler, and delivers over in form the instrument of his office, with the necessary charge on that occasion; after which he addresses the members of the lodge as follows:

'Brethren,

'Such is the nature of our constitution, that as some must of necessity rule and teach, so others must of course learn to submit and obey. Humility in both is therefore an essential duty. The brethren I have appointed to support me in the government of this lodge, I hope, are too well acquainted with the principles of Masonry, and the rules of good breeding, to extend their power; and the other members are too sensible of the necessity of their appointment, and of too generous dispositions, to envy their preferment. From the knowledge I have of both, I make no doubt but we shall all unite in the grand design of being happy, and of communicating happiness.'

The Grand Master gives all the brethren joy of their officers, recommends harmony, and expresses his desire that their only contention will be a laudable emulation in cultivating the royal Art, and the social virtues. Upon which all the New Lodge bow together, and return thanks for the honour of the constitution.

The Grand Secretary proclaims the New Lodge three times, with the honours of Masonry. Flourish with horns each time.

A song is then sung with a grand chorus. After which the New Master proceeds to explain the lodge.

The Grand Master orders the lodge to be registered in the Grand Lodge book, and the Grand Secretary to notify the same to all other regular lodges.

A song * concludes the ceremony, and the lodge is closed with the usual

---

* Many of the songs and anthems, used upon this and other occasions, are inserted at the end of this volume.

solemnities in the different degrees, by the Grand Master and his Officers; after which they return in procession to the apartment from whence they came.

This is the usual ceremony observed by regular masons, but the Grand Officers can abridge or extend it at pleasure.

The Ceremony observed at laying the Foundation Stones of Public Structures.

THIS ceremony is conducted by the Grand Master and his Officers, assisted by the members of the Grand Lodge. No private member, or inferior officer of a private lodge, is admitted to join in the ceremony. Provincial Grand Masters are authorized to execute this trust, in their several provinces, accompanied with their Officers, and the Masters and Wardens of the several Lodges under their jurisdiction. The chief magistrate and other civil officers of the place where the building is to be erected are generally solicited to attend on the occasion. The ceremony is thus conducted:

At

At the time appointed, the Grand Lodge is convened at some convenient place approved by the Grand Master. An excellent band of martial music is provided, and the brethren appear, in the insignia of the Order, elegantly dressed, with white gloves and aprons. The lodge is opened by the Grand Master, and the rules for regulating the procession to and from the place where the ceremony is to be performed are read by the Grand Secretary. The necessary cautions being given from the chair, the lodge is adjourned, and the procession begins in the following order:

Two Tylers, with drawn swords;
Music;
Members of the Grand Lodge, two and two;
A Tyler, in his uniform;
Past Grand Stewards;
Grand Tyler;
Present Grand Stewards, with white rods;
Secretary of the Stewards' Lodge;
Wardens of the Stewards' Lodge;
MASTER of the Stewards' Lodge;
Choiristers;

Choiristers;
Swordbearer, with the sword of state;
Grand Secretary, with his bag;
Grand Treasurer, with his staff;
Provincial Grand Masters;
Past Grand Wardens;
Past Deputy Grand Masters;
Past Grand Masters;
Chief Magistrate of the place;
Grand Wardens;
Deputy Grand Master;
Grand Chaplain;
The Bible, Square, and Compass on a crimson velvet cushion, carried by the Master of the oldest lodge, supported by two Stewards with white rods;
GRAND MASTER.
Two Stewards close the procession.

A triumphal arch is erected at the place where the ceremony is to be performed, with proper scaffolding for the reception of the brethren. The procession passes through the arch, and the brethren repair to their stands, while the Grand Master and his Officers take their places on a temporary

temporary platform covered with carpets. The Grand Master commands silence, and an ode on Masonry is sung. The necessary preparations are then made for laying the Stone, on which is engraved the year of our Lord and of Masonry, the name of the reigning Sovereign, the Grand Master's titles, &c. The Stone being raised up by means of an engine set up for that purpose, the Grand Chaplain repeats a short prayer, and the Grand Secretary, by the Grand Master's command, places under the Stone various sorts of coin and medals. Solemn music strikes up, an anthem is sung, and the Stone is let down into its place, and properly fixed; upon which the Grand Master descends to the Stone, and gives three knocks with his hiram, amidst the joyful acclamations of the spectators. The Grand Master re-ascends the platform, and an oration suitable to the occasion is delivered. A voluntary subscription is made for the workmen, and the sum collected is placed upon the

Stone by the Grand Treasurer. A song in honour of Masonry concludes the ceremony. The procession then returns to the place from whence it set out, the lodge is closed by the Grand Wardens, and an elegant entertainment is provided for the company.

The Ceremony observed at Funerals, according to ancient Custom: with the Service used on those occasions.

No mason can be interred with the formalities of the Order, unless by his own especial request, communicated to the Master of the lodge, of which he died a member; nor unless he had been advanced to the third degree of Masonry [*].

The Master of the lodge, on receiving intelligence of his death, and being made acquainted with the day and hour appointed for his funeral, is to issue his

[*] Foreigners and sojourners are excepted.

command

command for summoning the lodge; and immediately to make application, by the Grand Secretary, to the Deputy Grand Master, for a legal power and authority to attend the procession, with his officers, and such brethren as he may approve of, properly clothed †.

The

---

† By an express law of the Grand Lodge, it is enacted, ' That no regular mason do attend any ' funeral, or other public procession, clothed with ' the badges and ensigns of the Order; unless a dis- ' pensation for that purpose, has been obtained from ' the Grand Master, or his Deputy: under the ' penalty of forfeiting all the rights and privileges ' of the society; and of being deprived of the be- ' nefit of the general fund of charity, should he be ' reduced to want.'

As dispensations for public processions are seldom or never granted but upon very particular occasions, it cannot be thought that these will be very frequent, or that regular masons will incline to infringe an established law, by attending those which are not properly authorized. Many public parades under this character, it is true, have been made of late years; but it may safely be affirmed, that they never received the sanction of the Grand Master, or the countenance of any regular mason, conversant with the laws of the Society. Of this

the

The dispensation being obtained, the Master may invite as many lodges as he thinks proper, and the members of the said lodges may accompany their officers in form; but the whole ceremony must be under the direction of the Master of the lodge to which the deceased belonged; and he, and his officers, must be duly honoured, and cheerfully obeyed on the occasion.

All the brethren, who walk in procession, should observe, as much as possible, an uniformity in their dress. Decent

the public may be easily convinced, if they reflect that the reputation of the whole fraternity would be at risk by irregularity on such an occasion. It cannot be imagined, that the Grand Master, who is generally of noble birth, would so far degrade the dignity of his office, as to hazard the character of the society at large, by granting a dispensation from our established rules, for a public procession upon so trifling an occasion as a private benefit at a playhouse, public garden, or other place of general resort; where neither the interest of the fraternity, nor the public good, is concerned; and which, though it may be of advantage to one or two individuals, can never redound to the good of Masonry, or the honour of its patrons.

mourning,

mourning, with white stockings, gloves, and aprons*, is most suitable and becoming. No person ought to be distinguished with a jewel, unless he is an officer of one of the lodges invited to attend in form, and the officers of such lodges should be ornamented with white sashes and hatbands; as also the officers of the lodge to whom the dispensation is granted, who should likewise be distinguished with white rods.

In the procession to the place of interment, the different lodges rank according to their seniority; the junior ones preceding. Each lodge forms one division, and the following order is observed:

The Tyler, with his sword;
The Stewards, with white rods;
The Brethren out of office, two and two;
The Secretary, with a roll;
The Treasurer, with his badge of office;
Senior and Junior Wardens, hand in hand;
The Pastmaster;
The Master;

---

* This is the usual clothing of master-masons.

The Lodge to which the deceased Brother belonged, in the following order; all the members having flowers or herbs in their hands:

The Tyler;
The Stewards;
The Music [Drums muffled, and Trumpets covered];
The Members of the Lodge;
The Secretary and Treasurer;
The Senior and Junior Wardens;
The Pastmaster;
The Bible and Book of Constitutions on a cushion, covered with black cloth, carried by a Member of the Lodge;
The MASTER;
The Choiristers, singing an anthem;
The Clergyman;

| Pall Bearers, | The BODY, with the regalia placed thereon, and two swords crossed. | Pall Bearers; |

Chief Mourner;
Assistant Mourners;
Two Stewards;
A Tyler;

One or two lodges march, before the proceſſion begins, to the church-yard, to prevent confuſion, and make the neceſſary preparations. The brethren are on no account to deſert their ranks, or change their places, but keep in their different departments. When the proceſſion arrives at the gate of the church-yard, the lodge to which the deceaſed brother belonged, and all the reſt of the brethren, muſt halt, till the members of the different lodges have formed a perfect circle round the grave, when an opening is made to receive them. They then march up to the grave; and the clergyman, and the officers of the acting lodge, taking their ſtation at the head of the grave, with the choiriſters on each ſide, and the mourners at the foot, the ſervice is rehearſed, an anthem ſung, and that particular part of the ceremony is concluded with the uſual forms. In returning from the funeral, the ſame order of proceſſion is to be obſerved.

The Funeral Service.

The lodge is opened by the Master of the lodge to which the deceased belonged in the third degree, with the usual forms, and an anthem is sung. The body being placed in the center on a couch, and the coffin in which it is laid being open, the Master proceeds to the head of the corpse, and the service begins.

MASTER. 'What man is he that liv-
'eth, and shall not see death? shall he
'deliver his soul from the hand of the
'grave?

'Man walketh in a vain shadow, he
'heapeth up riches, and cannot tell who
'shall gather them.

'When he dieth, he shall carry no-
'thing away; his glory shall not descend
'after him.

'Naked we came into the world, and
'naked we must return: the Lord gave,
'and the Lord hath taken away; blessed
'be the name of the Lord.'

The grand honours are then given, and certain forms used, which cannot be here explained. Solemn music is introduced, during which the Master strews herbs or flowers over the body; and, taking the SACRED ROLL in his hand, he says,

'Let me die the death of the righteous,
'and let my last end be like his.'

The Brethren answer,

'God is our God, for ever and ever;
'he will be our guide even unto death.'

The Master then puts the roll into the chest; after which he says,

'Almighty Father, into thy hands
'we commend the soul of our loving
'brother.'

The Brethren answer three times, giving the grand honours each time,

'The will of God is accomplished;
'so be it.'

The Master then repeats the following prayer:

'Most glorious God, author of all
'good, and giver of all mercy, pour down
'thy blessings upon us, and strengthen
'all

'all our solemn engagements with the
'ties of fraternal affection. Let this
'striking instance of mortality remind
'us of our approaching fate; and
'so fit and prepare us for that awful
'period, whenever it may arrive, that
'after our departure hence, in peace and
'in thy favour, we may be received into
'thine everlasting kingdom, and there
'enjoy, in endless fruition, the just re-
'wards of a pious and virtuous life.
'Amen.'

An anthem being sung, the Master retires to the pedestal, and the coffin is shut up. An oration suitable to the occasion is then delivered; and the Master recommending love and unity, the brethren join hands, and renew to each other their pledged vows. The lodge is adjourned, and the procession begins, in the form already described, to the church, and from thence to the place of interment; where the following exhortation is given:

'The present occasion presents to our
'view a striking instance of the uncer-
'tainty

' tainty of life, and demonstrates the va-
' nity of all human pursuits. As the last
' offices paid to the dead are only useful
' as they are lectures to the living, we
' ought to derive instruction from them,
' and consider every solemnity of this
' kind as a summons to prepare for our
' approaching dissolution.

' Notwithstanding the various me-
' mentos of mortality with which we daily
' meet, notwithstanding we are convinced
' that Death has established his empire
' over all the works of Nature, yet,
' through some unaccountable infatua-
' tion, we are still apt to forget we were
' born to die. We go on from one de-
' sign to another, add hope to hope, and
' lay out plans for the subsistence and em-
' ployment of many years, till we are
' suddenly alarmed with the approach of
' Death when we least expected him, and
' at an hour which we had probably con-
' cluded to be the meridian of our existence.

' What are all the externals of majesty,
' the pride of wealth, or charms of beauty,
' when

'when Nature claims her juft debt? Let
' us, for a moment, throw our eyes on
' the laft fcene, view life ftript of her
' ornaments, and expofed in her natural
' meanness, and we fhall then be con-
' vinced of the futility of thefe empty de-
' lufions. In the grave, all fallacies are
' detected, all ranks are levelled, and all
' diftinctions are done away.

' As, therefore, life is uncertain, and
' all earthly purfuits are vain, let us no
' longer poftpone the important concern
' of preparing for eternity. Let us em-
' brace the happy moment while time
' and opportunity offer, in providing with
' care againft that great change, when the
' tranfitory pleafures of this world can no
' longer delight us, and the reflections of
' a life fpent in the exercife of piety and
' virtue yield the only comfort and con-
' folation.

' While we drop the fympathetic tear
' over the grave of our deceafed friend,
' let charity induce us to throw a veil
' over his foibles, whatever they may have
' been,

' been, and let us not with-hold from his
' memory the praife his virtues may have
' claimed. Suffer the apologies of human
' nature to plead in his behalf. Perfec-
' tion has never been attained, and the
' wifeſt as well as the beſt of men have
' erred. His meritorious actions let us
' imitate, and from his weakneſs derive
' inſtruction.

'Let the example of his fate excite
' our ſerious confideration, and ſtrengthen
' our reſolutions of amendment, leſt our
' expectations be alſo fruſtrated, and we
' be hurried unprepared into the preſence
' of an all-wife and powerful Judge, to
' whom the ſecrets of all hearts are known,
' and from whoſe dread tribunal no cul-
' prit can eſcape.

' To conclude: Let us ſupport with
' propriety the character of our profeſſion
' on every occaſion, advert to the nature
' of our ſolemn engagements, and ſup-
' plicate the divine grace to enable us to
' purſue with unwearied aſſiduity the ſa-
' cred tenets of our Order. Thus we
' ſhall

'shall secure the favour of that eternal
'Being whose goodness and whose power
'can know no bound; and prosecute
'our journey, without dread or appre-
'hension, to a far-distant country from
'which no traveller returns. By the light
'of the divine countenance, we shall pass
'without trembling through those gloomy
'mansions where all things are forgotten,
'and at that great and tremendous day,
'when, arraigned at the bar of divine
'justice, judgment shall be pronounced
'in our favour, we shall receive the
'reward of our virtue by acquiring the
'possession of an immortal inheritance,
'where joy flows in one continued stream,
'and no mound can check its course.'

The following invocations are then made by the Master, and the usual honours accompany each.

MASTER. 'May we be true and faithful, and may we live and die in love!'

ANSWER. 'So mote it be.'

MASTER. 'May we always profess what is good, and may we always act agreeably to our profession!'

ANSWER. ' So mote it be.'

MASTER. ' May the Lord bleſs us, 'and proſper us; and may all our good 'intentions be crowned with ſucceſs!'

ANSWER. ' So mote it be.'

The Secretaries then advance, and throw their rolls into the grave with the uſual forms, while the Maſter repeats with an audible voice:

' Glory be to God on high, on earth ' peace, and good-will towards men.'

ANSWER. ' So mote it be now, from ' henceforth, and for evermore.'

The Maſter then concludes the ceremony at the grave in the following words:

' From time immemorial it has been ' an eſtabliſhed cuſtom among the mem-
' bers of this reſpectable ſociety, when
' requeſted by a brother, to accompany
' his corpſe to the place of interment;
' and there to depoſit his remains with
' the uſual formalities.

' In conformity with this laudable ' uſage, and at the ſpecial requeſt of ' our

' our deceased brother, whose memory
' we revere, and whose loss we now de-
' plore, we are here assembled, under le-
' gal dispensation, in the form and charac-
' ter of masons, to resign his body to
' the earth from whence it came, and to
' offer up the last tribute of our fraternal
' affection and regard to his memory;
' thereby demonstrating to the world the
' sincerity of our past esteem, and our
' steady attachment to the principles of
' our honourable Order.

' With all proper respect to the esta-
' blished customs of the country in which
' we reside, with due deference to our su-
' periors in church and state, and with
' unlimited good-will to all mankind,
' we here appear in the character of our
' profession.—Invested with the badges
' of our sacred institution, we humbly
' implore the blessing of Heaven on all
' our zealous endeavours for the general
' good of society, and pray for our steady
' perseverance in the principles of piety
' and virtue.

' As

'As it has pleased the great Creator to remove our worthy brother now deceased, from the cares and troubles of a tranfitory exiftence, to a ftate of eternal duration; and thereby to weaken the chain by which we are linked one to another: may this example of the uncertainty of human life remind us of our approaching fate, and may we who furvive him, be more ftrongly cemented with the ties of union and friendfhip; and fo regulate our conduct here, by the facred dictates of truth and wifdom, as to enjoy, in the latter period of life, that ferene tranquillity of mind which ever flows from a clear and unfullied confcience, void of offence.

'Unto the grave we have refigned the body of our loving friend and brother, there to remain until the general refurrection; in favourable expectation that his immortal foul will then partake of thofe joys which have been prepared for the righteous from the beginning of the world: and we earneftly pray

'Almighty

'Almighty God, of his infinite goodnefs, at the grand tribunal of unbiaffed juftice, to extend his mercy towards him, and all of us, and to crown our felicity with everlafting blifs in the expanded realms of a boundlefs eternity. This we beg, for the honour of his holy name, to whom be glory, now and for ever. Amen.'

Thus the fervice ends, when the ufual honours are given, and the proceffion returns to the place from whence it came.

The brethren being all arrived at the lodge, the neceffary duties are complied with, and the bufinefs of Mafonry is renewed. The *regalia*, and ornaments of the deceafed, if an officer of a lodge, are returned to the Mafter in due form, and with the ufual ceremonies; after which the charges for regulating the conduct of the fraternity are rehearfed, and the lodge is clofed in the third degree with a bleffing.

THE
PRINCIPLES
OF
MASONRY
EXPLAINED.

In a Letter from the learned Mr. JOHN LOCKE, to the Right Hon. THOMAS Earl of PEMBROKE.

TO WHICH ARE ADDED,

Remarks and Annotations by the EDITOR.

ADVERTISEMENT.

THIS letter inclofes a copy of an old Manufcript in the Bodleian library, on the fubject of Free-Mafonry, in which the fundamental principles of that inftitution are accurately ftated. It is enriched with many learned notes and obfervations by Mr. Locke, who, though not at that time enrolled in the order of mafons, yet offers conjectures on the hiftory and traditions of Mafonry, which are not only juft but truly judicious.

Every reader muft feel fome fatisfaction in the perufal of this ancient manufcript, efpecially the true and faithful mafon, whom it more nearly concerns. The recommendation of the celebrated Mr. Locke, a philofopher of as great merit and penetration as this nation has ever produced, added to the real value of the piece itfelf, muft not only give it a fanction, but render it deferving a ferious and candid examination.

THE
PRINCIPLES
OF
MASONRY
EXPLAINED.

A Letter from the learned Mr. John Locke, to the Right Hon. Thomas Earl of Pembroke, with an old Manuscript on the subject of Free-Masonry.

MY LORD,   6th May, 1696.

I Have at length, by the help of Mr. Collins, procured a copy of that MS. in the Bodleian library, which you were so curious to see: and, in obedience to your Lordship's commands, I herewith send it to you. Most of the notes annexed

nexed to it, are what I made yesterday for the reading of my lady Masham, who is become so fond of Masonry, as to say, that she now more than ever wishes herself a man, that she might be capable of admission into the fraternity.

The MS. of which this is a copy, appears to be about 160 years old; yet (as your lordship will observe by the title) it is itself a copy of one yet more ancient by about 100 years: for the original is said to have been the hand-writing of K. Henry VI. Where that prince had it, is at present an uncertainty; but it seems to me to be an examination (taken perhaps before the king) of some one of the brotherhood of masons; among whom he entered himself, as it is said, when he came out of his minority, and thenceforth put a stop to a persecution that had been raised against them: But I must not detain your lordship longer by my preface from the thing itself.

I know not what effect the sight of this old paper may have upon your lordship;

ship; but for my own part I cannot deny, that it has so much raised my curiosity, as to induce me to enter myself into the fraternity, which I am determined to do (if I may be admitted) the next time I go to London, and that will be shortly. I am,

My Lord,

Your Lordship's most obedient,

And most humble servant,

JOHN LOCKE.

Certayne Queſtyons, wyth Anſweres to the ſame, concerning the Myſtery of Maçonrye; *writtene by the hande of kynge* Henrye, *the ſixthe of the name, and faythfullye copied by me* (1) Johan Leylande, *Antiquarius, by the commaunde of his* (2) *Highneſſe.*

They be as followethe,

Quest. What mote ytt be? (3)

Answ. Ytt beeth the ſkylle of nature, the underſtondynge of the myghte that ys hereynne, and its ſondrye werckynges; ſonderlyche,

———

(1) John Leylande was appointed by Henry VIII. at the diſſolution of monaſteries, to ſearch for, and ſave ſuch books and records as were valuable among them. He was a man of great labour and induſtry.

(2) His Highnesse, meaning the ſaid king Henry VIII. Our kings had not then the title of majeſty.

(3) What mote ytt be?] That is, what may this myſtery of maſonry be? The anſwer imports, that it conſiſts in natural, mathematical, and mechanical

sonderlyche, the skylle of rectenyngs, of waightes and metynges, and the treu manere of faconnynge al thynges for mannes use; headlye, dwellinges, and buyldynges of alle kindes, and al odher thynges that make gudde to manne.

Quest. Where dyd ytt begyne?

Answ. Ytt dyd begynne with the (4) fyrste menne in the este, whych were before the (5) ffyrste manne of the weste, and comynge westlye, ytt hathe broughte herwyth alle comfortes to the wylde and comfortlesse.

chanical knowledge. Some part of which (as appears by what follows) the masons pretend to have taught the rest of mankind, and some part they still conceal.

(4) (5) *Fyrste menne yn the este, &c.*] It should seem by this that masons believe there were men in the east before Adam, who is called the ' ffyrste manne of the weste;' and that arts and sciences began in the east. Some authors of great note for learning have been of the same opinion; and it is certain that Europe and Africa (which, in respect to Asia, may be called western countries) were wild and savage, long after arts and politeness of manners were in great perfection in China, and the Indies.

Quest. Who dyd brynge ytt weftlye?

Answ. The (6) Venetians, whoo beynge grate merchaundes, comed ffyrfte ffromme the efte ynn Venetia, for the commodytye of marchaundyfynge beithe efte and wefte, bey the redde and myddlelonde fees.

Quest. Howe comede ytt yn Engelonde?

Answ. Peter Gower (7) a Grecian, journeyedde ffor kunnynge yn Egypte, and

---

(6) *The Venetians, &c.*] In the times of monkifh ignorance it is no wonder that the Phenicians fhould be miftaken for the Venetians. Or, perhaps, if the people were not taken one for the other, fimilitude of found might deceive the clerk who firft took down the examination. The Phenicians were the greateft voyagers among the ancients, and were in Europe thought to be the inventors of letters, which perhaps they brought from the eaft with other arts.

(7) *Peter Gower.*] This muft be another miftake of the writer. I was puzzled at firft to guefs who Peter Gower fhould be, the name being perfectly Englifh; or how a Greek fhould come by fuch a name: But as foon as I thought of Pythagoras, I could fcarce forbear fmiling, to find that philofopher

and yn Syria, and yn everyche londe whereas the Venetians hadde plauntedde maconrye, and wynnynge entraunce yn al lodges of maçonnes, he lerned muche, and retournedde, and woned yn Grecia Magna (8) wackſynge, and becommynge

pher had undergone a metempſychoſis he never dreamt of. We need only conſider the French pronunciation of his name, Pythagore, that is Petagore, to conceive how eaſily ſuch a miſtake might be made by an unlearned clerk. That Pythagoras travelled for knowledge into Egypt, &c. is known to all the learned; and that he was initiated into ſeveral different orders of prieſts, who in thoſe days kept all their learning ſecret from the vulgar, is as well known. Pythagoras alſo made every geometrical theorem a ſecret, and admitted only ſuch to the knowledge of them, as had firſt undergone a five years ſilence. He is ſuppoſed to be the inventor of the 47th propoſition of the firſt book of Euclid, for which, in the joy of his heart, it is ſaid he ſacrificed a hecatomb. He alſo knew the true ſyſtem of the world, lately revived by Copernicus; and was certainly a moſt wonderful man. See his life by Dion. Hal.

(8) Grecia Magna, a part of Italy formerly ſo called, in which the Greeks had ſettled a large colony.

a myghtye

a myghtye (9) wyſeacre, and greatelyche renowned, and her he framed a grate lodge at Groton (10), and maked many maconnes, ſome whereoffe dyd journeye yn Fraunce, and maked manye maçonnes, wherefromme, yn proceſſe of tyme, the arte paſſed yn Engelonde.

Quest. Dothe maconnes diſcouer there artes unto odhers?

Answ. Peter Gower, whenne he journeyedde to lernne, was ffyrſte (11) made, and anonne techedde; evenne ſoe ſhulde

---

(9) Wyſeacre.] This word at preſent ſignifies ſimpleton, but formerly had a quite contrary meaning. Weiſager, in the old Saxon, is philoſopher, wiſeman, or wizard, and having been frequently uſed ironically, at length came to have a direct meaning in the ironical ſenſe. Thus Duns Scotus, a man famed for the ſubtilty and acuteneſs of his underſtanding, has, by the ſame method of irony, given a general name to modern dunces.

(10) Groton.] Groton is the name of a place in England. The place here meant is Crotona, a city of Grecia Magna, which in the time of Pythagoras was very populous.

(11) Fyrſte made.] The word MADE I ſuppoſe has a particular meaning among the maſons; perhaps it ſignifies, initiated.

all

all odhers beyn recht. Nathelefs (12) maçonnes hauethe always yn everyche tyme, from tyme to tyme, communycatedde to mannkynde foche of ther fecrettes as generallyche myghte be ufefulle; they haueth keped backe foche allein as fhulde be harmefulle yff they comed yn euylle haundes, oder foche as ne myghte be holpynge wythouten the techynges to be joynedde herwythe in the lodge, oder foche as do bynde the freres more ftrongelyche togeder, bey the proffytte and commodytye comynge to the confrerie herfromme.

Quest. Whatte artes haueth the maçonnes techedde mankynde?

(12) Maconnes haueth communycatedde, &c.] This paragraph hath fomething remarkable in it. It contains a juftification of the fecrecy fo much boafted of by mafons, and fo much blamed by others; afferting that they have in all ages difcovered fuch things as might be ufeful, and that they conceal fuch only as would be hurtful either to the world or themfelves. What thefe fecrets are, we fee afterwards.

Answ.

Answ. The artes (13) agricultura, architectura, aftronomia, geometria, numeres, mufica, poefie, kymiftrye, governmente, and relygyonne.

Quest. Howe commethe maçonnes more teachers than odher menne?

Answ. The hemfelfe haueth allein in (14) arte of fyndinge neue artes, whyche arte the ffyrfte maçonnes receaued from Godde; by the whyche they fyndethe whatte artes hem plefethe, and the treu

---

(13) *The artes, agricultura,* &c.] It feems a bold pretence this of the mafons, that they have taught mankind all thefe arts. They have their own authority for it; and I know not how we fhall difprove them. But what appears moft odd is, that they reckon religion among the arts.

(14) *Arte of ffyndinge neue artes.*] The art of inventing arts, muft certainly be a moft ufeful art. My lord Bacon's Novum Organum is an attempt towards fomewhat of the fame kind. But I much doubt, that if ever the mafons had it, they have now loft it; fince fo few new arts have been lately invented, and fo many are wanted. The idea I have of fuch an art is, that it muft be fomething proper to be applied in all the fciences generally, as algebra is in numbers, by the help of which, new rules of arithmetic are, and may be found.

way of techynge the fame. Whatt odher menne dothe ffynde out, ys onelyche bey chaunce, and herfore but lytel I tro.

Quest. What dothe the maconnes concele and hyde?

Answ. They concelethe the art of ffyndynge neue artes, and thattys for here own proffytte, and (15) preife: They concelethe the art of kepynge (16) fecrettes, thatt foe the worlde mayeth nothinge concele from them. Thay concelethe the art of wunderwerckynge, and of forefayinge thynges to comme, that fo

(15) Preife.] It feems the mafons have great regard to the reputation as well as the profit of their order; fince they make it one reafon for not divulging an art in common, that it may do honour to the poffeffors of it. I think in this particular they fhew too much regard for their own fociety, and too little for the reft of mankind.

(16) Arte of keepynge fecrettes.] What kind of an art this is, I can by no means imagine. But certainly fuch an art the mafons muft have: For though, as fome people fuppofe, they fhould have no fecret at all, even that muft be a fecret which being difcovered would expofe them to the higheft ridicule: and therefore it requires the utmoft caution to conceal it.

thay

thay fame artes may not be ufedde of the wyckedde to an euyell ende. Thay alfo concelethe the (17) arte of chaunges, the wey of wynnynge the facultye (18) of Abrac, the fkylle of becommynge gude and parfyghte wythouten the holpynges of fere and hope; and the univerfelle (19) longage of maconnes.

QUEST.

(17) Arte of chaunges.] I know not what this means, unlefs it be the tranfmutation of metals.

(18) Facultye of Abrac.] Here I am utterly in the dark.

(19) Univerfelle longage of maconnes.] An univerfal language has been much defired by the learned of many ages. It is a thing rather to be wifhed than hoped for. But it feems the mafons pretend to have fuch a thing among them. If it be true, I guefs it muft be fomething like the language of the Pantomimes among the ancient Romans, who are faid to be able, by figns only, to exprefs and deliver any oration intelligibly to men of all nations and languages. A man who has all thefe arts and advantages, is certainly in a condition to be envied: But we are told, that this is not the cafe with all mafons; for though thefe arts are among them, and all have a right and an opportunity to know them, yet fome want capacity, and others induftry to acquire them. However, of
all

Quest. Wylle he teche me thay fame artes?

Answ. Ye fhalle be techedde yff ye be warthye, and able to lerne.

Quest. Dothe all maçonnes kunne more then odher menne?

Answ. Not fo. Thay onlyche haueth recht and occafyonne more then odher menne to kunne, butt manye doeth fale yn capacity, and manye more doth want induftrye, thatt ys perneceffarye for the gaynynge all kunnynge.

Quest. Are maçonnes gudder menne then odhers?

Answ. Some maçonnes are not fo vertuous as fome odher menne; but, yn the mofte parte, thay be more gude than they woulde be yf thay war not maçonnes.

all their arts and fecrets, that which I moft defire to know is, 'The fkylle of becommynge gude and parfyghte;' and I wifh it were communicated to all mankind, fince there is nothing more true than the beautiful fentence contained in the laft anfwer, 'That the better men are, the more they love one another.' Virtue having in itfelf fomething fo amiable as to charm the hearts of all that behold it.

Quest.

QUEST. Doth maçonnes love eidther odher myghtylye as beeth fayde?

ANSW. Yea verylyche, and yt may not odherwife be: For gude menne and treu, kennynge eidher odher to be foche, doeth always love the more as thay be more gude.

Here endethe the queftyonnes, and awnfweres.

A GLOSSARY, *to explain the old words in the foregoing Manufcript.*

Allein, only
Alweys, always
Beithe, both
Commodytye, conveniency
Confrerie, fraternity
Faconnynge, forming
Fore fayinge, prophecying
Freres, brethren
Headlye, chiefly
Hem plefethe, they pleafe
Hemfelfe, themfelves
Her, there, their
Hereyune, therein
Herwyth, with it
Holpynge, beneficial

Kunne,

Kunne, know
Kunnynge, knowledge
Make gudde, are beneficial
Metynges, measures
Mote, may
Myddlelonde, Mediterranean
Myghte, power
Occasyonne, opportunity
Oder, or
Onelyche, only
Pernecessarye, absolutely necessary
Preise, honour
Recht, right
Reckenyngs, numbers
Sonderlyche, particularly
Skylle, knowledge
Wacksynge, growing
Werck, operation
Wey, way
Whereas, where
Woned, dwelt
Wunderwerckynge, working miracles
Wylde, savage
Wynnynge, gaining
Ynn, into

Remarks on the preceding MS. and on the Annotations of Mr. LOCKE.

This dialogue possesses a double claim to our regard; first for its antiquity, and next for the notes added to it by so great a man as Mr. Locke: but Mr. Locke being then a stranger to the fraternity, is a circumstance that it is hoped will render a few additional remarks not altogether impertinent.

The conjectures of this ingenious and learned annotator concerning it being an examination taken before King Henry of some one of the fraternity of masons, are just. The severe edict passed at that time against the society, and the discouragement given to the masons by the bishop of Winchester and his party, induced that prince, in his riper years, to make a stricter scrutiny into the nature of the masonic institution. This was fortunately attended with the happy circumstance of gaining his favour, together with his patronage. Had not the disturbances and civil commotions in the kingdom, during his reign, folely attracted the notice of government, it is more than probable this act would have been repealed, through the interceffion of the duke of Gloucefter; whofe attachment to the fociety was particularly confpicuous.

Page 154. What mote ytt be?] Mr. LOCKE obferves, in his annotation on this queftion, that the anfwer to it imports, that Mafonry confifts of natural, mathematical, and mechanical knowledge; fome part of which, he fays, the mafons *pretend* to have taught the reft of mankind, and fome part they ftill conceal.—The arts which have been communicated to the world by mafons, are particularly fpecified in an anfwer to one of the following queftions; as are alfo thofe which they have reftricted to themfelves for wife purpofes.—Morality, however, might likewife have been included in this anfwer, as it conftitutes a principal part of the mafonic fyftem.

Page 155. Where dyd ytt begyne?] In the annotation on the anfwer to this queftion, question, Mr. Locke seems to suggest, that masons believe there were men in the east before Adam, which is indeed a mere conjecture. This opinion may be confirmed by many learned authors, but masons comprehend the true meaning of Masonry taking rise in the east, and spreading to the west, without having recourse to Præadamites. East and west are terms peculiar to 'the society, and, when masonically adopted,· are only intelligible to the fraternity; as they refer to certain forms and established customs among themselves.

Page 156. Who dyd brynge ytt westlye?] The judicious correction of an illiterate clerk, in the answer to this question as well as the next, reflects great credit on the ingenious annotator. His explanation is just, and his elucidation accurate.

Page 156. Howe comede ytt yn Engelonde?]. The records of the fraternity inform us, that Pythagoras was regularly initiated

initiated into Masonry; and being properly instructed in the mysteries of the Art, he was much improved, and propagated the principles of the Order in other countries into which he afterwards travelled.

Page 158. Dothe maçonnes discouer here artes unto odhers?] Masons, in all ages, have studied the general good of mankind. Every art which is useful, or necessary for the support of authority and preservation of good government, as well as for promoting science, they have cheerfully communicated to mankind. Those matters which were of no public importance, they have carefully preserved in their own breasts; such as, the tenets of the Order, their mystic forms, and particular customs. These are only of private use to distinguish each other in different countries, and thus to confine their privileges to the just and meritorious.

Page 159. Whatte artes haueth the maçonnes techedde mankynde?] The arts which the masons have publicly taught, are here specified. It appears to have surprised the learned annotator, that religion should be ranked among the arts propagated by the fraternity. Masons have ever, in compliance with the tenor of their profession, paid due obedience to the moral law, and have inculcated its precepts with powerful energy on all their followers. The doctrine of one God, the creator and preserver of the universe, has always been their firm belief. Under the influence of this doctrine, the conduct of the fraternity has been regulated through a succession of ages. The progress of knowledge and philosophy, aided by divine revelation, having abolished many of the vain superstitions of antiquity, and enlightened the minds of men with the knowledge of the true God and the sacred mysteries of the christian faith, masons have always acquiesced in, and zealously pursued every measure which might promote that holy religion, so wisely calculated to make men happy. In those countries,

countries, however, where the gospel has not reached, and christianity displayed her beauties, the masons have pursued the universal religion, or the religion of nature; that is, to be good men and true, by whatever denomination or persuasion they have been distinguished. A cheerful compliance with the established religion of the country in which they live, so far as it corresponds with, and is agreeable to the tenets of Masonry, is earnestly recommended in all their assemblies. This universal conformity, notwithstanding private sentiment and opinion, answers the laudable purpose of conciliating true friendship among men, and may be considered as an art few are qualified to learn, and still fewer to teach.

Page 160. How commethe maçonnes more teachers than odher menne?] The answer implies, that masons, having greater opportunities of improving their talents, are better qualified to instruct others. Mr. Locke's observation on their having the art of finding new arts, is very judicious, and his explanation seems to be just. The fraternity have ever made the study of the arts a principal part of their private amusement; in their several assemblies nice and difficult theories have been faithfully canvassed and wisely explained; fresh discoveries have also been produced, and those already known have been accurately illustrated. The different classes established, the gradual progression of knowledge communicated, and the regularity observed throughout the whole system of their government, is an evident proof of this assertion. Those initiated into the mysteries of the Art soon discover that masons are possessed of the art of finding out new arts; to which knowledge they gradually arrive by instruction from, and familiar intercourse with, men of genius and ability.

Page 161. What dothe the maçonnes concele and hyde?] The answer imports, the art of finding new arts, for their profit

profit and praife; and then particularizes the different arts they carefully conceal. Mr. Locke's remark, that this shews too much regard for their own society, and too little for the reft of mankind, is rather fevere, when he has admitted the propriety of concealing from the world what is of no real public utility, left, being converted to bad ufes, the confequences might be prejudicial to fociety. By the word *praife*, is here meant honour and refpect, to which mafons were entitled, and which only could give credit to the wife doctrines they propagated. Their fidelity has given them a claim to efteem, and the rectitude of their manners has demanded veneration.

Of all the arts which the mafons profefs, the art of fecrecy particularly diftinguifhes them. Taciturnity is a proof of wifdom, and is of the utmoft importance in the different tranfactions of life. Sacred, as well as profane hiftory [*],

has

[*] Many inftances may be adduced from hiftory, of the great veneration that was paid to this art by

has declared it to be an art of ineftimable value. Secrecy is agreeable to the Deity the ancients. Pliny informs us, that Anaxarchus, being imprifoned with a view to extort from him fome fecrets with which he had been entrufted, and dreading that exquifite torture might induce him to betray his truft, bit his tongue in the middle, and threw it in the face of Nicocreon, the tyrant of Cyprus.—No torments could make the fervants of Plancus betray the fecrets of their mafter; with fortitude they encountered every pain, and ftrenuoufly fupported their fidelity, till death put a period to their fufferings.—The Athenians had a ftatue of brafs, to which they bowed; the figure was reprefented without a tongue to denote fecrecy.—The Egyptians worfhipped Harpocrates, the god of filence, who was always reprefented holding his finger at his mouth.—The Romans had likewife their goddefs of filence, named Angerona, to whom they offered worfhip.—Lycurgus, the celebrated lawgiver, as well as Pythagoras, the great fcholar, particularly recommended this virtue: efpecially the laft, who kept his difciples filent during five years, that they might learn the valuable fecrets he had to communicate unto them; thereby expreffing that fecrecy was the rareft, as well as the nobleft art.

The following ftory is related by a Roman hiftorian, which, as it may be equally pleafing and inftructive, I fhall here infert at full length.

The fenators of Rome had ordained, that, during their confultations in the fenate-houfe, each fenator

Deity himself, who gives the glorious example, by concealing from mankind the secrets

nator should be permitted to bring his son with him, who was to depart if occasion required; but this favour was not general, being restricted only to the sons of noblemen; who were tutored from their infancy in the virtue of secrecy, and thereby qualified, in their riper years, to discharge the most important offices of government with fidelity and wisdom. About this time it happened, that the senators met on a very important case, and the affair requiring mature deliberation, they were detained longer than usual in the senate-house, and the conclusion of their determinations adjourned to the following day; each member engaging, in the mean time, to keep secret the transactions of the meeting. Among other noblemen's sons, who had attended on the occasion, was the son of the grave Papyrus; a family of great renown and splendor. The young Papyrus was no less remarkable for his genius, than for the prudence of his deportment. On his return home, his mother, anxious to know what important case had been debated in the senate that day, which had detained the senators so long beyond the usual hour, entreated him to relate the particulars. The noble and virtuous youth told her, it was a business not in his power to reveal, he being solemnly enjoined to silence. On hearing this, her importunities were more earnest, and her inquiries more minute. Intelligence she must have;

secrets of his providence. The wiseſt of men cannot pry into the arcana of heaven, nor

all evaſions were vain. By fair ſpeeches and entreaties, with liberal promiſes, ſhe endeavoured to break open this little caſket of ſecrecy; but theſe means proving ineffectual, ſhe adopted rigorous meaſures, and had recourſe to ſtripes and violent threats; firmly perſuaded that force would extort, what lenity could not effect. The youth, finding his mother's threats to be very harſh, but her ſtripes more ſevere; comparing his love to her, as his mother, with the duty he owed to his father; the one mighty, but the other impulſive; lays her and her fond conceit in one ſcale; his father, his own honour, and the ſolemn injunctions to ſecrecy in the other ſcale; and finding the latter greatly preponderate, with a noble and heroic ſpirit preſerved his honour, at the riſk of his mother's diſpleaſure; and thus endeavoured to relieve her anxiety:

'Madam, you may well blame the ſenate for
'their long ſitting, at leaſt for preſuming to call in
'queſtion a caſe ſo truly impertinent; except the
'wives of the ſenators are allowed to conſult on it,
'there can be no hope of a concluſion. I ſpeak
'this only from my own opinion; I know their
'gravity will eaſily confound my juvenile appre-
'henſions; yet, whether nature or duty inſtructs
'me to do ſo, I cannot tell. It ſeems neceſſary to
'them, for the increaſe of people, and the public
'good, that every ſenator ſhould be allowed two
'wives;

nor can they divine to-day what to morrow may bring forth.

'wives; or otherwise, their wives two husbands. I shall hardly incline to call, under one roof, two men by the name of father; I had rather with cheerfulness salute two women by the name of mother. This is the question, Madam; and tomorrow it is to be determined.'

His mother hearing this, and he seeming unwilling to reveal it, she took it for an infallible truth. Her blood was quickly fired, and rage ensued. Without inquiring any farther into the merits of the case, she immediately dispatched messengers to all the other ladies and matrons of Rome, to acquaint them of this weighty affair now under deliberation in the senate, in which the peace and welfare of their whole lives were so nearly concerned. The melancholy news soon spread a general alarm; and a thousand conjectures were formed. The ladies being resolved to give their assistance in the decision of this weighty point, immediately assembled. Headed by young Papyrus's mother, on the next morning, they proceeded to the senate-house. Though it is remarked that a parliament of women are seldom governed by one speaker, yet the affair being urgent, the haste pertinent, and the case (on their behalf) of the utmost consequence, the revealing woman must speak for all the rest. It was agreed, that she should insist on the necessity of the concurrence of the senators' wives

Mr. Locke has made several judicious observations on the answer to this question.

to the determination of a law in which they were so particularly interested. When they came to the door of the senate-house, such a noise was made, for admission to sit with their husbands in this grand consultation, that all Rome seemed to be in an uproar. Their business, however, must be known before they could gain an audience. This being complied with, and their admission granted, such an elaborate oration was made by the female speaker on the occasion, in behalf of her sex, as astonished the whole senators. She requested, that the matter might be seriously canvassed according to justice and equity; and expressed the determined resolutions of all her sisters, to oppose a measure so unconstitutional, as that of permitting one husband to have two wives, who could scarcely please one. She proposed, in the name of her sisters, as the most effectual way of peopling the state, that if any alteration was made in the established custom of Rome, women might be permitted to have two husbands. The senators were soon informed of Papyrus's scheme to preserve his reputation, and on the riddle being solved, the ladies were greatly confounded, and departed with blushing cheeks. The noble youth, who had thus proved himself worthy of his trust, was highly commended for his fidelity; but, in order to avoid a like tumult in future, it was resolved, that the custom of introducing

tion. His being in the dark concerning the meaning of the faculty of Abrac, I am no ways surprised at, nor can I conceive how he could otherwise be. ABRAC is an abbreviation of the word ABRACADABRA. In the days of ignorance and superstition, that word had a magical signification. The explanation of it is now lost.

Our celebrated annotator has taken no notice of the masons having the art of working miracles, and foresaying things to come. Astrology was received as one of the arts which merited their patronage; and the good effects resulting from the study of it, may fully vindicate the coun-

ducing the sons of the senators should be abolished. Papyrus, however, on account of his attachment to his word, and his discreet policy, was excepted from this restriction, and ever afterwards freely admitted into the senate-house, where many honours were conferred upon him.

The virtue and fidelity of Papyrus is indeed worthy of imitation; but the masons have still a more glorious example in their own body, of a brother, accomplished in every art, who, rather than forfeit his honour, or betray his trust, fell a sacrifice to the cruel hand of a barbarous assassin.

tenance given by the masons to this delusion.

The ancient philosophers applied with unwearied diligence to discover the aspects, magnitudes, distances, motions, and revolutions of the heavenly bodies; and according to the discoveries they made, pretended to foretell future events, and to determine concerning the secrets of providence: Hence this study grew, in a course of time, to be a regular science, and was admitted among the other arts practised by masons.

Astrology, it must be owned, however vain and delusive in itself, has proved extremely useful to mankind, by promoting the excellent science of astronomy. The vain hope of reading the fates of men, and the success of their designs, has been one of the strongest motives to induce them, in all countries, to an attentive observation of the celestial bodies; whence they have been taught to measure time, to mark the duration of seasons, and to regulate the operations of agriculture.

Page 163. Wylle he teche me thay fame artes?] By the anfwer to this queftion, we learn the neceffary qualifications which are required in a candidate for Mafonry; a good character, and an able capacity.

Page 163. Dothe all maçonnes kunne more then odher menne?] The anfwer only implies, that though mafons have a better opportunity than the reft of mankind, of improving in ufeful knowledge, a want of capacity in fome, and of application in others, obftructs their progrefs.

Page 163. Are maçonnes gudder menne then odhers?] Mafons are not underftood to be more virtuous in their lives and actions, than other men may be; but it is an undoubted fact, that a ftrict conformity to the rules of their profeffion, may make them better men than they otherwife would be.

Page 164. Dothe maçonnes love eidher odher myghtylye as beeth fayde?] The anfwer to this queftion is truly great, and is judiciously remarked upon by the learned annotator.

By the answers to the three last questions, Masonry is vindicated against all the objections of cavillers; its excellency is displayed; and every censure against it, on account of the transgressions of its professors, entirely removed. No bad man can be enrolled in our records, if known to be so; but should he impose upon us, and we unwarily are led to receive him, our endeavours are exerted to reform him: and, it is certain, by being a mason, he will become a better subject to his sovereign, and a more useful member to the state.

Upon the whole, Mr. Locke's observations on this curious manuscript, are well deserving a serious and careful examination; and there remains little doubt, but the favourable opinion this philosopher conceived of the society of masons before his admission, was sufficiently confirmed after his initiation.

THE HISTORY OF MASONRY IN ENGLAND.

ADVERTISEMENT.

IN the First Edition we confined our remarks on the history of Masonry to a particular period, and inserted a detail of the principal transactions which then occurred. To render this part of the Book more complete, we have now extended our plan, and traced the progress of Masonry from its first appearance in Britain, to the present time.

THE
HISTORY
OF
MASONRY.

THE hiftory of Britain, previous to the invafion of the Romans, is fo mixed with fable, as not to afford any fatisfactory account either of the original inhabitants of the ifland, or of the arts practifed by them. It appears, however, from the writings of the beft hiftorians, that they were not deftitute of genius or tafte. There are yet in being the remains of fome ftupendous works executed by them much earlier than the time of the Romans, and thefe veftiges of antiquity, though defaced by the cruel hand of time, difplay no fmall fhare of ingenuity in the invention,

invention, and are convincing proofs that the science of Masonry was not unknown in those rude ages.

The Druids are said to have retained many usages among them similar to those of masons, but of what they chiefly consisted, we cannot, at this distance of time, with certainty, discover. These philosophers held their assemblies in woods and groves, and observed the most impenetrable secrecy in explaining their principles and opinions, which being known only to themselves, must have perished with them.

The Druids were the priests of the Britons, Gauls, and other Celtic nations. They were divided into three classes; the bards, who were poets and musicians, formed the first class; the vates, who were priests and physiologists, composed the second class; and the third class consisted of the Druids, who added moral philosophy to the study of physiology.

It is suggested that the Druids derived their system of government from Pythagoras.

goras. Study and speculation were the favourite pursuits of these philosophers. In their private retreats they entered into a disquisition of the origin, laws, and properties of matter, the form and magnitude of the universe, and even the most sublime and hidden secrets of nature. On these subjects they formed a variety of hypotheses, which they delivered to their disciples in verse, that they might more easily retain them in memory, being bound by oath not to write them.

In this manner the Druids communicated their peculiar tenets, and under the veil of mystery concealed every branch of useful knowledge. This secured to their order universal admiration and respect, while their religious instructions were every where received with reverence and submission. To them was committed the education of youth, and from their seminaries many valuable productions issued. They determined all causes, both ecclesiastical and civil; they taught philosophy, astrology, politics, rites, and ceremonies;

and

and in songs recommended the heroic deeds of great men to the imitation of posterity.

It would be contrary to the intention of this treatise to enlarge further on the usages that prevailed among these ancient philosophers; on these we can offer but probable conjectures; it will therefore be more prudent to abbreviate our observations on this head, and, leaving the experienced mason to make his own reflections on their affinity to the masonic rites, hasten to relate occurrences of more importance and better authenticated.

Upon the arrival of the Romans in Britain, arts and sciences began to flourish apace. In the progress of civilization, Masonry came into esteem, and was much encouraged by Cæsar, and several of the Roman generals, who succeeded him in the government of this island. At this period the masons, though few in number, were remarkably distinguished for their skill in architecture. We find them employed in erecting walls, forts, bridges, cities, temples, palaces, courts of juftice, and other ftately works. Hiftory, however, is filent concerning their lodges or conventions, and tradition affords but an imperfect account of their ufages and cuftoms.

The wars which foon after broke out between the conquerors and the conquered obftructed the progrefs of Mafonry in Britain, and the Art continued in a low ftate till the arrival of the Emperor Caraufius, when, under his aufpices, it revived. This general, having fhaken off the Roman yoke, contrived every means to render his perfon and government acceptable to the people. As he poffeffed real merit, he encouraged learning and learned men, improved the country in the civil arts, and intended to have eftablifhed an empire in Britain. He collected workmen and artificers from all parts, and under his fway they enjoyed peace and tranquillity. He held the mafons in great veneration, and appointed Albanus, his fteward, principal fuperintendant

tendant over their assemblies. Under this patron, the lodges or conventions of the fraternity were regularly conducted. The masons, through the influence of Albanus, obtained a charter from Carausius to hold a general council, at which this worthy knight presided in person as Grand Master, and assisted at the reception of many persons. To this council the name of Assembly was afterwards given*. Albanus was born at

---

* An old MS. which was destroyed with many others in 1720, said to have been in the possession of Nicholas Stone, a curious sculptor under Inigo Jones, contained the following particulars:

'St. Alban loved masons well, and cherished
' them much, and made their pay right good; for
' he gave them ijs. per weeke, and iijd. to their
' cheer †; whereas, before that time in all the land,
' a mason had but a penny a day, and his meat, un-
' til St. Alban mended itt. And he gott them a
' charter from the King and his counsell for to hold
' a general counsell, and gave itt to name Assemblie.
' Thereat he was himselfe, and did helpe to make
' masons, and gave them good charges.'

† A MS. written in the reign of James II. before cited in this volume, contains an account of this circumstance, and increases the weekly pay to 3 s. 6 d. and 3 d. a day for the bearers of burdens.

Verulam,

Verulam, (now St. Albans, in Hertfordshire) of a noble family. In his youth he travelled to Rome, where he served seven years under the Emperor Dioclesian. On his return home, by the example and persuasion of Amphibalus of Caer-leon (now Chester), who had accompanied him in his travels, he was converted to the Christian faith, and in the tenth and last persecution of the Christians, was beheaded A. D. 303. He was the first who suffered martyrdom for the Christian religion in Britain, of which the venerable Bede gives the following account. The Roman governor having been informed that St. Alban harboured a Christian in his house, he sent a party of soldiers to apprehend Amphibalus. St. Alban immediately put on the habit of his guest *, and presented himself to the officers.

* The garment which Alban wore upon this occasion was called a *Caracalla*; it was a kind of cloak with a cowl, resembling the vestment of the Jewish priests. Walsingham relates, that it was preserved in a large chest in the church of Ely, which

officers. He was carried before a magistrate, where he behaved with such a manly freedom, and so powerfully supported the cause of his friend, as not only to incur the displeasure of the judge, but to bring upon himself the punishment above specified.

The old constitutions affirm that St. Alban was employed by Carausius to environ the city of Verulam with a wall, and to build him a fine palace; and that the Emperor, as a reward for his diligence in executing these works, appointed him steward of his household, and chief ruler of the realm. However this may be, there is great reason to believe, from the corroborating testimonies of ancient histo-

---

which was opened in the reign of Edward II. A. D. 1314; and Thomas Rudburn, another writer of equal authority, confirms this relation, and adds, That there was found with this garment an old Writing in these words: 'This is the Caracalla of 'St. Amphibalus, the monk and preceptor of St. 'Alban; in which that proto-martyr of England 'suffered death, under the cruel persecution of 'Dioclesian against the Christians.'

rians,

rians, that this knight was a celebrated architect, and a great encourager of good workmen. It cannot then be supposed that Free-masonry should be neglected under such a patron.

After the departure of the Romans from Britain, Masonry made but a slow progress, and was in a little time almost totally neglected. The irruptions of the Picts and Scots obliged the southern inhabitants of the island to solicit the assistance of the Saxons, to repel these invaders. As the Saxons increased, the native Britons sunk into obscurity, and, ere long, yielded the superiority to their protectors, and acknowledged their sovereignty and jurisdiction. These rough and ignorant heathens, despising every thing but war, soon put a finishing stroke to all the remains of ancient learning which had escaped the fury of the Picts and Scots. They continued their depredations, with unrestrained rigour, till the arrival of some pious teachers from Wales and Scotland, when many of these savages were reconciled to Chriſtianity, and the doctrines of that religion gained ground among them. As Chriſtianity ſpread, Maſonry was eſtabliſhed, and lodges began to be formed*. Theſe lodges, being under the direction of foreigners, were ſeldom convened, and never attained any degree of conſideration or importance.

Maſonry continued in this ſituation till the year 557, when Auſtin, with forty more monks, among whom the ſciences had been preſerved, came into England. Auſtin was commiſſioned by Pope Gregory, to baptize Ethelbert King of Kent, who appointed him the firſt archbiſhop of Canterbury. This monk and his aſſociates propagated the principles of the Chriſtian faith among the inhabitants of Britain, and by their influence, in little more than ſixty years, all the kings of the heptarchy were converted. The lodges now began to flouriſh under the patronage of Auſtin, and ſeveral foreigners came into England who introduced the Gothic

* See the Book of Conſtitutions.

ſtyle

style of building among the masons. Austin appeared at the head of the fraternity in founding the old cathedral of Canterbury in 600, and the cathedral of Rochester in 602.

Several expert masons arrived in England from France in 680, who formed themselves into lodges, under the direction of Bennet, abbot of Wirral, who was appointed by Kenred, king of Mercia, to inspect their proceedings.

During the heptarchy, however, Masonry continued in a low state. In the year 856 it revived under the patronage of St. Swithin, who was employed by Ethelwolph, the Saxon king, to repair some pious houses, and gradually improved till the reign of Alfred, A. D. 872, when, in the person of that prince, it found a zealous protector.

Masonry has, for the most part, kept pace with the progress of learning, and we have generally found the patrons and encouragers of the latter most remarkable for cultivating and promoting the former.

former. No prince ever studied more to polish and improve the understandings of his subjects than Alfred, and therefore no one could prove a better friend to Masonry. By his indefatigable assiduity in the pursuit of knowledge, he induced his people to imitate his example, and thereby reformed their dissolute and barbarous manners. Hume, in his history of Great Britain relates the following particulars of this prince:

Alfred usually divided his time into three equal portions; one was employed in sleep, and the refection of his body by diet and exercise; another in the dispatch of business; and a third in study and devotion. That he might more exactly measure the hours, he made use of burning tapers of equal lengths, which he fixed in lanthorns; an expedient suited to that rude age when the geometry of dialing and the mechanism of clocks and watches were totally unknown. By this regular distribution of his time, though he often laboured under great bodily infirmities,

OF MASONRY. 197

firmities, this martial hero, who fought in person fifty-six battles by sea and land, was able, during a life of no extraordinary length, to acquire more knowledge and even to compose more books, than most studious men, blest with greater leisure and application, have, in more fortunate ages, made the object of their uninterrupted industry.

This prince was not negligent in encouraging the mechanical arts. Masonry, therefore, claimed a great part of his attention. He invited, from all quarters, industrious foreigners to repeople his country, which had been laid desolate by the ravages of the Danes. He introduced and encouraged manufactures of all kinds among them; no inventor or improver of any ingenious art did he suffer to go unrewarded; and he set apart a seventh part of his revenue for maintaining a number of workmen, whom he constantly employed in rebuilding his ruined cities, castles, palaces, and monasteries. The university of Oxford was founded by him.

him. On his death in 900, Edward succeeded to the throne.

During the reign of Edward, the masons continued to hold their lodges, under the sanction of Ethred, his sister's husband, and Ethelward, his brother, to whom he intrusted the care of the fraternity. Ethelward was a prince of great learning, and an able architect. He founded the university of Cambridge.

Edward died in 924, and was succeeded by Athelstane his son, who appointed his brother Edwin patron of the masons. This prince procured a charter from Athelstane, empowering them to meet annually in communication at York. In this city the first Grand Lodge of England was formed in 926, at which Edwin presided as Grand Master *. Here many old writings were produced in Greek, Latin,

---

* A record of the society, written in the reign of Edward IV. said to have been in the possession of the famous Elias Ashmole, founder of the Museum at Oxford, and unfortunately destroyed, with other papers on the subject of Masonry, at the Revolution,

Latin, and other languages, from which, it is said, the constitutions of the English lodges have been extracted. Athelstane kept

volution, gives the following account of the state of Masonry at this period.

'That though the ancient records of the Brother-
'hood in England were many of them destroyed or
'lost in the wars of the Saxons and Danes, yet
'King Athelstane, (the grandson of King Alfred
'the Great, a mighty architect) the first anointed
'king of England, and who translated the Holy
'Bible into the Saxon tongue, (A. D. 930) when
'he had brought the land into rest and peace, built
'many great works, and encouraged many masons
'from France, who were appointed overseers there-
'of, and brought with them the charges and regu-
'lations of the lodges, preserved since the Roman
'times; who also prevailed with the King to im-
'prove the constitution of the English lodges ac-
'cording to the foreign model, and to increase the
'wages of working masons.

'That the said King's brother, Prince Edwin,
'being taught Masonry, and taking upon him the
'charges of a master mason, for the love he had to
'the said Craft, and the honourable principles
'whereon it is grounded, purchased a free charter
'of King Athelstane, for the masons having a cor-
'rection among themselves, (as it was anciently ex-
'pressed) or a freedom and power to regulate them-
'selves, to amend what might happen amiss, and

'to

kept his court for some time at York, where he received several embassies from foreign princes, with rich presents of various kinds. He was loved, honoured, and admired by all the princes of Europe, who sought his friendship and courted his alliance. He was a mild sovereign, a kind brother, and a true friend. The only blemish that historians find in the whole reign of Athelstane, is the supposed murder of his brother Edwin. This youth was distinguished for his virtues, and having died two years before his brother, a false report was spread of his be-

'to hold a yearly communication and general as-
'sembly.

'That accordingly Prince Edwin summoned all
'the masons in the realm to meet him in a congre-
'gation at York, who came and composed a gene-
'ral lodge, of which he was Grand Master; and
'having brought with them all the writings and
'records extant, some in Greek, some in Latin,
'some in French, and other languages, from the
'contents thereof that assembly did frame the con-
'stitution and charges of an English lodge, made a
'law to preserve and observe the same in all time
'coming, and ordained good pay for working ma-
'sons, &c.'

ing wrongfully put to death by him. But this action is so improbable in itself, so inconsistent with the character of Athelstane, and indeed so slenderly attested, as to be undeserving of a place in history *.

The

---

* The excellent writer of the life of King Athelstane †, has given so clear and so perfect a view of this event, that the reader cannot receive greater satisfaction than in that author's own words.

The business of Edwin's death, is a point the most obscure in the story of this King, and, to say the truth, not one even of our best historians, hath written clearly, or with due attention, concerning it. The fact, as commonly received, is this: The King suspecting his younger brother Edwin, of designing to deprive him of his crown, caused him, notwithstanding his protestations of innocency, to be put on board a leaky ship, with his armour-bearer and page. The young prince, unable to bear the severity of the weather, and want of food, desperately drowned himself. Some time after, the King's cup-bearer, who had been the chief cause of this act of cruelty, happened, as he was serving the King at table, to trip with one foot, but recovering himself with the other, ' See,' said he pleasantly, ' how brothers afford each other ' help ;' which striking the King with the remembrance of what himself had done, in taking off

* Biog. Brit. vol. i. p. 63.

The activity and princely conduct of Edwin qualified him, in every respect, to preside over so celebrated a body of men

Edwin, who might have helped him in his wars, he caused that business to be more thoroughly examined, and finding his brother had been falsely accused, caused his cup-bearer to be put to a cruel death, endured himself seven years sharp penance, and built the two monasteries of Middleton and Michelness, to atone for this base and bloody fact *.

Dr. Howel, speaking of this story, treats it as if very indifferently founded, and, on that account, unworthy of credit †. Simeon of Durham, and the Saxon chronicle, say no more, than that Edwin was drowned by his brother's command, in the year 933 ‡. Brompton places it in the first, or at farthest in the second year of his reign; and he tells us the story of the rotten ship, and of his punishing the cup-bearer §. William of Malmsbury, who is very circumstantial, says, he only tells us what he heard ‖; but Matthew, the flower-gatherer ╪, stamps the whole down as an indubitable truth. Yet these discordant dates are not to be accounted for. If he was drowned in the second, he could not be alive in the tenth year of the King, the first is the more probable date, because about that time there cer-

---

* Speed's Chronicle, Book vii. chap. 38.   † Gen. Hist. P. iv. c. 2. § 10.   ‡ Simeon Dunelm. p. 154. Chron. Saxon. p. 111.   § Chronicon. p. 828.   ‖ De Gest. R. A. lib. ii.   ╪ Matth. Florileg.

tainly

men as the masons. Under him they were employed in repairing and building many churches and other edifices, which had been destroyed by the ravages of the Danes and other invaders, not only in the city of York, but at Beverley, and other places. On the death of Edwin, Athelstane undertook the direction of the lodges,

tainly was a conspiracy against King Athelstane, in order to dethrone him, and put out his eyes, yet he did not put the author of it to death; is it likely then that he should order his brother to be thrown into the sea upon bare suspicion? But the reader must remember, that we cite the same historians, who have told us this story, to prove that Athelstane was unanimously acknowledged King, his brethren being too young to govern; one would think then, they could not be old enough to conspire. If we take the second date, the whole story is destroyed; the King could not do seven years penance, for he did not live so long; and as for the tale of the cupbearer, and his stumbling at the King's table, the same story is told of Earl Godwin, who murdered the brother of Edward the Confessor. Lastly, nothing is clearer from history, than that Athelstane was remarkably kind to his brethren and sisters, for whose sakes he lived single, and therefore one would think his brother had less temptation to conspire against him.

and propagated the art of Masonry in peace and security.

When Athelstane died, the masons dispersed, and continued in an unsettled state till the reign of Edgar in 960, when they were again collected by St. Dunstan. Under the auspices of this patron they were employed in rearing some pious structures, but meeting with little encouragement, their lodges soon declined. After Edgar's death, Masonry remained in a low condition upwards of fifty years. It began to revive under the patronage of Edward the Confessor, in 1041, and several great works were executed by this prince. He rebuilt Westminster Abbey, assisted by Leofrick, earl of Coventry, whom he had appointed to superintend the masons. The Abbey of Coventry, and many other structures, were also finished by this accomplished architect.

William the Conqueror acquired the crown of England in 1066: he appointed Gundulph, bishop of Rochester, and Roger de Montgomery, joint patrons of of the masons, who at this time excelled both in civil and military architecture. Under the auspices of these patrons, the fraternity were employed in building the Tower of London, which was completed in the reign of William Rufus, who rebuilt London bridge with wood, and first constructed the palace and hall of Westminster in 1087. On the accession of Henry I, the lodges continued to be held; and from this prince the first Magna Charta, or charter of liberties, was obtained by the Normans. Stephen succeeded Henry in 1135, and employed the fraternity in building a chapel at Westminster, now the House of Commons, and several other works. These were finished under the direction of Gilbert de Clare, marquis of Pembroke, who at this time presided over the lodges.

During the reign of Henry II. the grand master of the Knights Templars superintended the masons, and employed them in building their Temple in Fleet-street, A. D. 1155. Masonry continued under

under the patronage of this Order till the year 1199, when John succeeded his brother Richard in the crown of England. Peter de Colechurch was then appointed Grand Master. He began to rebuild London bridge with stone, which was finished by William Alcmain in 1209. Peter de Rupibus succeeded Peter de Colechurch in the office of Grand Master, and Geoffrey Fitz-Peter, chief surveyor of the king's works, acted as deputy under him. Masonry flourished under the auspices of these two artists, during the remainder of this and the following reign.

On the accession of Edward I. A. D. 1272, the care of the lodges was entrusted to Walter Giffard, archbishop of York; Gilbert de Clare, earl of Gloucester; and Ralph, lord of Mount Hermer, the progenitor of the family of the Montagues. These architects superintended the finishing of Westminster Abbey, which had been begun in 1220, during the minority of Henry III. In the reign of Edward II. the fraternity were employed in building

building Exeter and Oriel colleges, Oxford; Clare-hall, Cambridge; and many other structures; under the auspices of Walter Stapleton, bishop of Exeter, who had been appointed patron of the masons in 1307.

Masonry flourished in England in the reign of Edward III. This prince became the patron of science, and the encourager of literature. He applied with indefatigable assiduity to the constitutions of the Order; he revised and meliorated the ancient charges, and added several wise regulations to the original code of laws, by which the fraternity had been governed. He patronized the lodges, and appointed five deputies under him to inspect their proceedings, viz. 1. John de Spoulee, who rebuilt St. George's chapel at Windsor, where the order of the garter was first instituted, A. D. 1350; 2. William a Wickham, afterwards bishop of Winchester, who rebuilt the castle of Windsor at the head of 400 free-masons, A. D. 1357; 3. Robert a Barnham, who

finished

finished St. George's hall at the head of 250 free-masons, with other works in the castle, A. D. 1375; 4. Henry Yeuele, (called in the old records, the King's freemason) who built the Charter-house in London; King's hall, Cambridge; and Queenborough castle; and who also rebuilt St. Stephen's chapel, Westminster; and 5. Simon Langham, abbot of Westminster, who rebuilt the body of that cathedral as it now stands. From some old records still extant it appears, that at this period lodges were numerous, and that communications of the fraternity were held under the protection of the civil magistrate *.

Richard

---

* An old record of the Society runs thus:

'In the glorious reign of King Edward III. when
'lodges were more frequent, the Right Worshipful
'the Master and Fellows, with consent of the lords
'of the realm, (for most great men were then ma-
'sons) ordained,

'That for the future, at the making or admis-
'sion of a brother, the constitution and the ancient
'charges should be read by the Master or Warden.

'That

Richard II. having succeeded his grandfather Edward III. in 1377, William a Wickham was continued Grand Master. He

'That such as were to be admitted master-masons,
' or masters of work, should be examined whether
' they be able of cunning to serve their respective
' lords, as well the lowest as the highest, to the ho-
' nour and worship of the aforesaid art, and to the
' profit of their lords; for they be their lords that
' employ and pay them for their service and travel.'

The following particulars are also contained in a very old MS. of which a copy is said to have been in the possession of the late George Payne, Esq; Past Grand Master.

' That when the Master and Wardens meet in a
' lodge, if need be, the sheriff of the county, or the
' mayor of the city, or alderman of the town, in
' which the congregation is held, should be made
' fellow and sociate to the Master, in help of him
' against rebels, and for upbearing the rights of the
' realm.

' That entered prentices, at their making, were
' charged not to be thieves or thieves-maintainers;
' that they should travel honestly for their pay, and
' love their fellows as themselves, and be true to
' the king of England, and to the realm, and to the
' lodge.

' That at such congregations it shall be inquired,
' whether any master or fellow has broke any of the
' articles agreed to; and if the offender, being duly
' cited

He afterwards rebuilt Westminster-hall as it now stands; and employed the fraternity in building New College, Oxford, and Winchester college, both of which he founded at his own expence.

Henry, duke of Lancaster, taking advantage of Richard's absence in Ireland, got the parliament to depose him, and next year caused him to be murdered. Thus he supplanted his cousin, and mounted the throne by the name of Henry IV. He appointed Thomas Fitz Allen, earl of Surrey, Grand Master. In this reign the Guildhall of London was built. The King dying in 1413, Henry V. succeeded

'cited to appear, prove rebel, and will not attend,
' then the lodge shall determine against him, that he
' shall forswear (or renounce) his masonry, and shall
' no more use this craft, the which if he presume
' for to do, the sheriff of the county shall prison
' him, and take all his goods into the King's hands,
' till his grace be granted him and issued. For
' this cause principally have these congregations
' been ordained, that as well the lowest as the high-
' est should be well and truly served in this art fore-
' said, throughout all the kingdom of England.
' Amen, so mote it be.'

to the crown; when Henry Chicheley, archbishop of Canterbury, obtained the direction of the fraternity; and under the auspices of this patron, lodges and communications were frequent.

Henry VI. a minor, succeeding to the throne in 1422, the parliament endeavoured to disturb the masons, by passing the following act to prohibit their chapters and conventions:

3 Hen. VI. cap. 1. A. D. 1425.

Masons *shall not confederate in chapters or congregations.*

'Whereas, by the yearly congrega-
' tions and confederacies made by the
' masons in their general assemblies, the
' good course and effect of the statutes of
' labourers be openly violated and broken,
' in subversion of the law, and to the
' great damage of all the commons; our
' sovereign lord the King, willing in this
' case to provide a remedy, by the advice
' and consent aforesaid, and at the special
' request of the commons, hath ordained
' and

' and established, that such chapters and
' congregations shall not be hereafter
' holden; and if any such be made, they
' that cause such chapters and congrega-
' tions to be assembled and holden, if they
' thereof be convict, shall be judged for
' felons: and that the other masons, that
' come to such chapters or congregations,
' be punished by imprisonment of their
' bodies, and make fine and ransome at
' the king's will *.'

This

---

* Judge Coke gives the following opinion on this statute:

' All the statutes concerning labourers before this
' act, and whereunto this act doth refer, are repealed
' by the statute of 5 Eliz. cap. 4. about A. D. 1562,
' whereby the cause and end of making this act is
' taken away, and consequently the act is become of
' no force; for *cessante ratione legis, cessat ipsa lex:*
' and the indictment of felony upon this statute must
' contain, That those chapters and congregations
' are to the violating and breaking of the good
' course and effect of the statutes of labourers;
' which now cannot be so alleged, because these
' statutes be repealed. Therefore this would be
' put out of the charge of justices of the peace.'
INSTITUTES, Part III. fol. 19.

It

This act was never once put in force, nor the fraternity deterred from assembling as usual under archbishop Chicheley, who still continued to preside over them. Notwithstanding this rigorous edict, the effect of prejudice and malevolence in an arbitrary set of men, lodges were formed in different parts of the kingdom; and tranquillity, joy, and felicity reigned among the fraternity *.

It is plain, from the above opinion, that this act, though never expressly repealed, can have no force at present. The masons may rest very quiet, may continue to hold their assemblies, and may propagate their mysteries, as long as their conformity to their professed principles entitles them to the sanction of government. Masonry is too well known in this country, to raise any suspicion in the legislature. The greatest personages have presided over the society, and under their auspicious government, at different times, an acquisition of patrons, both great and noble, has been made. It would therefore be absurd to imagine, that any legal attempt will ever be thought of to disturb the peace and harmony of a society so truly respectable and so highly honoured.

* The Latin Register of William Molart, prior of Canterbury, in manuscript, pap. 88. entitled,
' Liberatio

As the attempt of parliament to suppress the lodges and communications of masons renders the transactions of this period worthy our attention, it may not be improper to state some of the circumstances which are supposed to have given rise to this severe edict.

The Duke of Bedford, at that time regent of the kingdom, being in France, the regal power was vested in his brother Humphrey, Duke of Gloucester *, who was

---

* 'Liberatio generalis Domini Gulielmi Prioris Ecclesiæ Christi Cantuariensis, erga Fastum Natalis Domini 1429,' informs us, that, in the year 1429, during the minority of this prince, a respectable lodge was held at Canterbury, under the patronage of Henry Chicheley, the archbishop; at which were present Thomas Stapylton, the Master; John Morris, custos de la lodge lathomorum, or warden of the lodge of masons; with fifteen fellow-crafts, and three entered apprentices, all of whom are particularly named.

* This prince is said to have received a more learned education than was usual in his age, to have founded one of the first public libraries in England, and to have been a great patron of learned men. If the records of the society may be relied on, we have

was styled protector and guardian of the kingdom. The care of the young king's person and education was entrusted to Henry Beaufort, bishop of Winchester, the Duke's uncle. The bishop was a prelate of great capacity and experience, but of an intriguing and dangerous character. As he aspired to the government of affairs, he had continual disputes with his nephew the protector, and gained frequent advantages over the vehement and impolitic temper of that prince. Being invested with power, he soon began to shew his pride and haughtiness, and he wanted not followers and agents, who were busy to augment his influence *.

The

---

have reason to believe, that he was particularly attached to the masons, that he was admitted into their Order, and that he assisted at the initiation of King Henry in 1442.

* In a parliament held at Westminster on the 17th of November 1423, to answer a particular end, it was ordained, ' That if any person, committed for ' grand or petty treason, should wilfully break out ' of prison, and escape from the same, it should be
' deemed

The animosity between the uncle and nephew daily increased, and the authority of

'deemed petty treason, and his goods be forfeited ‡. About this time, one William King, of Womolton in Yorkshire, servant to Sir Robert Scott, lieutenant of the Tower, pretended, that he had been offered by Sir John Mortimer, (cousin to the lately deceased Edward Mortimer, earl of March, the nearest in blood to the English crown, and then a prisoner in the Tower) ten pounds to buy him clothes, with forty pounds a year, and to be made an earl, if he would assist Mortimer in making his escape; that Mortimer said, he would raise 40,000 men on his enlargement, and would strike off the heads of the rich bishop of Winchester, the duke of Gloucester, and others. This fellow undertook to prove upon oath the truth of his assertion. A short time after, a scheme was formed to cut off Mortimer, and an opportunity soon offered to carry it into execution. Mortimer being permitted one day to walk to the Tower wharf, was suddenly pursued, seized, brought back, accused of breaking out of prison, and of attempting his escape. He was tried, and the evidence of King being admitted, was convicted, agreeably to the late statute, and afterwards beheaded.

The death of Mortimer occasioned great murmuring and discontent among the people, and

‡ Wolfe's Chronicle, published by Stowe.

of parliament, at length, was obliged to interpose. On the laſt day of April, 1425, the parliament met at Weſtminſter. The ſervants and followers of the peers coming thither, armed with clubs and ſtaves, occaſioned its being named THE BATT PARLIAMENT. Several laws were then made, and among the reſt, the act for aboliſhing the ſociety of maſons*; at leaſt for preventing their aſſemblies threatened a ſpeedy ſubverſion of thoſe in power. Many hints were thrown out, both in public and private aſſemblies, of the fatal conſequences which were expected to ſucceed this commotion. The amazing progreſs it made, juſtly alarmed the ſuſpicions of the ambitious prelate, who ſpared no pains to exert his power on the occaſion.

* Dr. Anderſon, in the firſt edition of the Book of Conſtitutions, in a note, makes the following obſervation on this act:

‘ This act was made in ignorant times, when
‘ true learning was a crime, and geometry con-
‘ demned for conjuration; but it cannot derogate
‘ from the honour of the ancient fraternity, who,
‘ to be ſure, would never encourage any ſuch con-
‘ federacy of their working brethren. By tradition
‘ it is believed, that the parliament were then too
‘ much influenced by the illiterate clergy, who
‘ were

blies and congregations. As their meetings were secret, it can raise no surprise that they should attract the attention of the aspiring prelate, renew his apprehension, and incur his displeasure †.

Sovereign

'were not accepted masons, nor understood archi-
' tecture, (as the clergy of some former ages) and
' were generally thought unworthy of this brother-
' hood. Thinking they had an indefeasible right
' to know all secrets, by virtue of auricular con-
' fession, and the masons never confessing any thing
' thereof, the said clergy were highly offended, and
' at first suspecting them of wickedness, represented
' them as dangerous to the state during that mino-
' rity, and soon influenced the parliament to lay
' hold of such supposed arguments of the working
' masons, for making an act that might seem to
' reflect dishonour upon even the whole fraternity,
' in whose favour several acts had been before and
' after that period made.'

† The bishop was diverted from his persecution of the masons, by an affair in which he was more nearly concerned. On the morning of St. Simon and Jude's day, after the lord mayor of London had returned to the city from Westminster, where he had been taking the usual charges of his high office, he received a special message, while seated at dinner, from the duke of Gloucester, requiring his immediate attendance. He immediately repaired

to

Sovereign authority, however, being vested in the duke of Gloucester, as protector to the palace, and being introduced into the presence, the duke commanded his lordship to see that the city was properly watched the following night, as he expected his uncle would endeavour to make himself master of it by force, unless some effectual means were adopted to stop his progress. This command was strictly obeyed; and, at nine o'clock the next morning, the bishop of Winchester, with his servants and followers, attempted to enter the city by the bridge, but were prevented by the vigilance of the citizens; who, having been previously apprized of their design, repelled them by force. This unexpected repulse enraged the haughty and imperious prelate, who immediately collected a numerous body of archers and other men at arms, and commanded them to assault the gate with shot. The citizens directly shut up their shops, and crowded to the bridge in great numbers, when a general massacre would certainly have ensued, had it not been for the timely interposition and prudent administration of the mayor and aldermen, who happily stopt all violent measures, and, in all probability, prevented a great effusion of blood.

The archbishop of Canterbury, and Peter, duke of Coimbra, eldest son of the King of Portugal, with several others, endeavoured to appease the fury of the two contending parties, and, if possible, to bring about a reconciliation between them; but all to no purpose, neither party would yield. They rode eight or ten times backwards and forwards,

tector of the realm, the execution of the laws, and all that related to the civil magistrate, centered in him: a fortunate circumstance for the masons at this critical juncture. The Duke, knowing them using every scheme they could think of to prevent further extremities, before they could succeed in their mediation, or bring the parties to a conformity; at last it was agreed on both sides, that all hostile proceedings should drop, and the matter be referred to the award of the duke of Bedford. Upon this, peace was restored, and the city remained in quiet for the present.

The bishop lost no time in transmitting his case to the duke of Bedford; and in order to gloss it over with the best colours, he wrote the following letter:

'Right high and mighty prince, and my right
'noble, and after one, leiuest [earthly] lord; I re-
'commend me unto your grace with all my heart.
'And as you desire the welfare of the King our sove-
'reign lord, and of his realms of England and
'France, your own weal [health] with all yours,
'haste you hither: For by my troth, if you tarry
'long, we shall put this land in jeopardy [adven-
'ture] with a field, such a brother you have here;
'God make him a good man. For your wisdom
'well knoweth that the profit of France standeth
'in the welfare of England, &c. The blessed
'Trinity keep you. Written in great haste at
'London,

them to be innocent of the accufations laid againſt them, not only protected them,

'London, on All-hallowen-even, the 31ſt of Octo-
'ber, 1425.
                'By your fervant, to my lives end,
                        'HENRY, WINCHESTER.'

This tremendous letter had the defired effect, and haſtened the return of the duke of Bedford to London, where he arrived on the 10th of January, 1425-6. On the 21ſt of February he held a great council at St. Albans, adjourned it to the 15th of March at Northampton, and the 25th of June at Leiceſter. Batts and ſtaves being now prohibited, the followers of the members of parliament attended with ſtones in a ſling, and plummets of lead. The duke of Bedford employed the authority of parliament to reconcile the differences which had broke out betwixt his brother and the biſhop of Wincheſter; and he obliged theſe rivals to promiſe before that aſſembly, that they would bury all quarrels in oblivion. Thus the long wiſhed for peace between theſe two great perſonages, was, to all appearance, accompliſhed.

The duke of Glouceſter, during the difcuſſion of this matter before parliament, exhibited the following charge, among five others, againſt the biſhop of Wincheſter: 'That he had, in his letter to the
'duke of Bedford at France, plainly declared his
'malicious purpoſe of aſſembling the people, and
'ſtirring up a rebellion in the nation, contrary to
'the king's peace.'

The biſhop's anſwer to this accuſation was, 'That
'he never had any intention to diſturb the peace of
                                                'the

them, but transferred the charge of rebellion, sedition, and treason, from them, to the bishop of Winchester, and his fol-

'the nation, or raise any rebellion; but that he
'sent to the duke of Bedford to solicit his speedy re-
'turn to England to settle all those differences which
'were so prejudicial to the peace of the kingdom:
'That though he had indeed written in the letter,
'*That if he tarried, we should put the land in ad-
'venture by a field, such a brother you have here*;
'he did not mean it of any design of his own, but
'concerning the seditious assemblies of masons,
'carpenters, tylers, and plaisterers; who, being
'distasted by the late act of parliament against the
'excessive wages of those trades, had given out
'many seditious speeches and menaces against cer-
'tain great men, which tended much to rebellion †:
'That the duke of Gloucester did not use his en-
'deavour, as he ought to have done in his place,
'to suppress such unlawful assemblies; so that he
'feared the king, and his good subjects, must have
'made a field to withstand them; to prevent which,
'he chiefly desired the duke of Bedford to come over.'

As the masons are unjustly suspected of having given rise to some of the civil commotions of this period, I thought it necessary to insert the foregoing particulars, in order to clear them from this false charge. Most of the circumstances here mentioned, are extracted from Wolfe's Chronicle published by Stowe.

† The above particulars are extracted from one of Elias Ashmole's MSS. on the subject of Free-masonry.

lowers;

lowers; who, he afferted, were the firft to difturb the public peace, and kindle the flames of civil difcord.

The bifhop of Winchefter, fenfible that his actions were not to be juftified by the laws of the land, prevailed with the King, through the interceffion of the parliament, whom his riches had particularly interefted in his favour, to grant him letters of pardon for all offences committed by him, contrary to the ftatute of provifors, and other acts of præmunire. Five years after this, he procured another pardon, under the great feal, for all forts of crimes whatever, from the creation of the world to the 26th of July 1437.

The Duke of Gloucefter, notwithftanding all the cardinal's precautions, in 1442, drew up frefh articles of impeachment againft him, and prefented them with his own hands to the King; defiring that judgment might be paffed upon him, according to his crimes. The king referred the matter to his council, who took it under their confideration; but, being principally

principally ecclesiastics, they favoured the cardinal. At last, the duke, wearied out with their tedious delays and fraudulent dealings, dropt the prosecution, and the cardinal escaped.

Nothing could remove the inveteracy * of the cardinal against the duke of Glou-

---

* The Bishop planned the following scheme at this time to irritate the duke of Gloucester: His dutchess, the daughter of Reginald lord Cobham, had been accused of the crime of witchcraft, and it was pretended that a waxen figure of the King was found in her possession; which she, and her associates, Sir Roger Bolingbroke, a priest, and one Margery Jordan of Eye, melted in a magical manner before a slow fire, with an intention of making Henry's force and vigour waste away by like insensible degrees. The accusation was well calculated to affect the weak and credulous mind of the King, and gain belief in an ignorant age. The dutchess was brought to trial, with her confederates, and the prisoners were pronounced guilty: the dutchess was condemned to do public penance in London for three days, and to suffer perpetual imprisonment; the others were executed.

The protector, provoked at such repeated insults offered to his dutchess, made a noble and stout resistance to these most abominable and shameless proceedings, but it unfortunately ended in his own destruction.

cester; he was resolved to destroy a man whose popularity might become dangerous, and whose resentment he had so much reason to apprehend. The Duke had ever been a strenuous opposer of every measure contrary to the public good. By his prudence, as well as the authority of his birth and station, he had prevented an absolute sovereign power from being vested in the King's person. This enabled Winchester to gain many partisans, who were easily brought to concur in the ruin of the prince.

In order to effectuate the plan the enemies of this prince had concerted to murder him, a parliament was summoned to meet at St. Edmondsbury in 1447, where they expected he would lie entirely at their mercy. As soon as he appeared, on the second day of the sessions, he was accused of treason, and thrown into prison; where he was found the next day, basely and shamefully murdered. It was pretended, that his death was natural; but though his body, which was exposed to public view, bore no marks of outward injury, no one doubted that he had fallen a facrifice to the vengeance of his enemies. Five of his fervants were tried for aiding him in his treafons, and condemned to be hanged, drawn, and quartered. They were hanged accordingly, cut down alive, ftripped naked, and marked with a knife to be quartered; when the marquis of Suffolk, through a mean and pitiful affectation of popularity, produced their pardon, and faved their lives: the moft barbarous kind of mercy that can poffibly be imagined!

Thus fell that great prince the duke of Gloucefter. His death was univerfally lamented throughout the whole kingdom. He had long obtained, and deferved well, the firname of GOOD. He was a lover of his country, a friend to good men, the protector of the mafons, a patron of the learned, and an encourager of every work worthy of everlafting memorial. His inveterate profecutor, the hypocritical bifhop, ftung with remorfe,

fcarce

scarce survived him two months; when, after a long life spent in falsehood and politics, he sunk into oblivion, with all the daggers of divine vengeance sticking in his heart *.

After the death of the cardinal the masons continued to hold their lodges

* The wickedness of the Cardinal's life, and his mean, base, and unmanly death, will ever be a bar against any vindication of his memory for the good which he did while alive, or which the money he had amassed could do after his decease. When in his last moments he was heard to utter these mean expressions: 'Why should I die, who am 'possessed of so much wealth? If the whole king-'dom could save my life, I am able by my policy 'to preserve it, or by my money to purchase it. 'Will not death be bribed, nor money do every 'thing?' The inimitable Shakespeare, after giving a most horrible picture of despair, and a tortured conscience, in the person of the cardinal, introduces King Henry to him with these sharp and piercing words:

'Lord cardinal, if thou think'st on heav'n's bliss,
'Lift up thy hand, make signal of that hope.'
——He dies, and makes no sign.
Hen. VI. Act 3.

'The memory of the wicked shall rot, but the un-'justly persecuted shall be had in everlasting remem-'brance.'

without dread or apprehension. The King being initiated into the Order in the year 1442, he was very intent on obtaining a thorough knowledge of the Art. He perufed the ancient charges*, revifed the conftitutions, and, with the confent of his council, prefided in perfon over the mafons. Many lords and gentlemen of the court followed his Majefty's ex-

---

* A record in the reign of Edward IV. runs thus: ‘ The company of mafons, being otherwife termed ‘ free-mafons, of auntient ftaunding and good reckoninge, by means of affable and kind meetyngs ‘ dyverfe tymes, and as a lovinge brotherhode ufe ‘ to doe, did frequent this mutual affembly in the ‘ tyme of Henry VI. in the twelfth yeare of his ‘ moft gracious reign, A. D. 1434.’ The fame record fays farther, ‘ That the charges and laws of ‘ the free-mafons have been feen and perufed by our ‘ late Soveraign King Henry VI. and by the lords ‘ of his moft honourable council, who have allowed ‘ them, and declared, That they be right good ‘ and reafonable to be holden, as they have been ‘ drawn out and collected from the records of auntient tymes,’ &c. &c.

From all which it appears, that before the troubles which happened in the reign of this unfortunate prince, free mafons were in high eftimation.

ample, and Masonry once more flourished in England*. The King nominated William Wanefleet, bishop of Winchester, Grand Master, who afterwards built Magdalene College, Oxford, and many other pious houses, at his own expence. Eton College, near Windsor, and King's College, Cambridge, were built under the

---

* While these transactions were carrying on in England, the masons were countenanced and protected in Scotland by King James I. After his return from captivity, he became the patron of the learned, and a zealous encourager of Masonry. The Scottish records relate, that he honoured the lodges with his royal presence; that he settled a yearly revenue of four pounds Scots (an English noble), to be paid by every master-mason in Scotland, to a Grand Master, chosen by the Grand Lodge, and approved by the crown, one nobly born, or an eminent clergyman, who had his deputies in cities and counties, and every new brother at entrance paid him also a fee. His office empowered him to regulate in the fraternity what should not come under the cognizance of law-courts. To him appealed both mason and lord, or the builder and founder, when at variance, in order to prevent law-pleas; and, in his absence, they appealed to his Deputy or Grand Warden, that resided next to the premises.

direction of Wanefleet. Henry also founded Christ's College, Cambridge; and his queen, Margaret of Anjou, Queen's College, in the same university.

Masonry continued to flourish in England till the peace of the kingdom was interrupted by the civil wars between the two royal houses of York and Lancaster, when it fell into an almost total neglect, and continued in that state till 1471, when it began to revive, under the auspices of Richard Beauchamp, bishop of Sarum. This prelate had been appointed Grand Master by Edward IV. and had been honoured with the title of chancellor of the garter for repairing the castle and chapel of Windsor.

During the short reigns of Edward V. and Richard III. Masonry was on the decline; but on the accession of Henry VII. A. D. 1485, it came again into esteem, under the patronage of the Master and fellows of the order of St. John at Rhodes (now Malta), who assembled their grand lodge in 1500, and chose Henry

Henry their protector. Under the royal aufpices the fraternity revived their affemblies, and Mafonry refumed its priftine fplendor. A grand lodge was formed in the palace, on the 24th of June 1502, at which the King prefided in perfon as Grand Mafter; and having appointed John Iflip, abbot of Weftminfter, and Sir Reginald Bray, knight of the garter, his wardens for the occafion, he proceeded in ample form to the eaft end of Weftminfter Abbey, and laid the foundation ftone of that famous piece of Gothic architecture, known by the name of Henry VII.'s Chapel. Under the direction of Sir Reginald Bray, the palace of Richmond was afterwards built, and many other ftately works.

Henry VIII. fucceeded his father in 1509, and appointed Cardinal Wolfey Grand Mafter. This prelate built Hampton Court, Whitehall, Chrift Church College, Oxford, and feveral other good edifices; all of which, upon his difgrace, were forfeited to the crown, A. D. 1530.

Thomas Cromwell, earl of Essex, succeeded the Cardinal in the office of Grand Master; and employed the fraternity in building St. James's Palace, Christ's Hospital, and Greenwich castle. In 1534 the King and parliament threw off allegiance to the pope of Rome. The King being declared supreme head of the church, no less than 926 pious houses were suppressed; many of which were afterwards converted into stately mansions for the nobility and gentry. Under the direction of John Touchet lord Audley, who, on Cromwell's being beheaded in 1540, had succeeded to the office of Grand Master, Masonry continued to flourish; and the fraternity were employed in building Magdalene College, Cambridge, and several other structures.

Edward VI. a minor, succeeding to the throne in 1547, his guardian and regent, Edward Seymour, duke of Somerset, undertook the management of the masons, and built Somerset-house in the Strand;

Strand; which, on his being beheaded, was forfeited to the crown in 1552. John Poynet, bishop of Winchester, then became the patron of the fraternity, and continued to preside over the lodges till the King died, A. D. 1553.

The masons remained without any nominal patron till the reign of Elizabeth, when Sir Thomas Sackville accepted the office of Grand Master. Lodges were held, however, during this period, in different parts of England, particularly at York, where the fraternity were both numerous and respectable. The following remarkable circumstance is recorded of Elizabeth: hearing that the masons were in possession of secrets, which they would not reveal, and being jealous of all secret assemblies, she sent an armed force to York, with intent to break up their annual communication. This design, however, was happily frustrated by the interposition of the Grand Master; who took care to initiate some of the chief officers she had sent on this duty. They

They joined in communication with the masons, and reported to the Queen, that the society consisted of a peculiar set of skilful architects, who cultivated arts and sciences, promoted peace and friendship, one with another, and never meddled in affairs of church or state. Upon which the Queen countermanded her orders, and never afterwards attempted to disturb the fraternity.

Sir Thomas Sackville having resigned in 1567, Francis Russel, earl of Bedford, was elected Grand Master in the North, and Sir Thomas Gresham (who built the Royal Exchange, in the South.) Charles Howard, earl of Effingham, succeeded Sir Thomas Gresham, and continued to preside over the lodges in the South till 1588, when George Hastings, earl of Huntingdon, accepted the office of Grand Master, in which station he continued till the Queen died in 1603.

On the death of Elizabeth, the crowns of England and Scotland were united in her successor, James VI. of Scotland, who was

OF MASONRY. 235

was proclaimed King of England, Scotland, and Ireland, on the 25th of March 1603. At this period Masonry flourished apace in both kingdoms, and the lodges were convened under the royal patronage. Several gentlemen of fine taste returned from their travels full of laudable emulation, if not to excel the Italian revivers, at least to imitate them in old Roman and Grecian Masonry. These ingenious travellers brought home some pieces of old columns, some curious drawings, and books of architecture. Among the number was the celebrated Inigo Jones, son of Inigo Jones, a citizen of London. He was put apprentice to a joiner, and had a natural taste for the art of designing. He was first renowned for his skill in landscape painting, and was patronized by the learned William Herbert, afterwards earl of Pembroke. He made the tour of Italy at his lordship's expence, where he improved under some of the best disciples of the famous Andrea Palladio. On his return to England, he
laid

laid aside the pencil, and confined his study to architecture. He became the Vitruvius of Britain, and the rival of Palladio. He was appointed General Surveyor to King James I. under whose royal auspices Masonry flourished. He was elected Grand Master mason of England, and was deputised by his Sovereign to preside over the lodges. During his administration, many learned men were initiated into Masonry, and the society was composed of respectable members. The most ingenious artists resorted to England, where they met with great encouragement. Lodges were constituted and formed into seminaries of instruction in the sciences and polite arts, after the design of the Italian schools. The quarterly communications of the Grand Lodge were revived, and the annual festivals regularly observed.

Inigo Jones continued to preside over the fraternity till the year 1618, when he was succeeded by the earl of Pembroke. Many eminent, wealthy, and learned men were

OF MASONRY. 237

were initiated under his lordship's auspices, and the mysteries of the Order were held in high estimation.

On the death of King James in 1615, Charles ascended the throne. The earl of Pembroke continued to preside over the fraternity till 1630, when he resigned in favour of Henry Danvers, earl of Danby, who was succeeded in 1633 by Thomas Howard, earl of Arundel, the progenitor of the Norfolk family. In 1635 Francis Russel, earl of Bedford, accepted the government of the society; but as Inigo Jones had, with indefatigable assiduity, continued to patronize the lodges, he was re-elected the following year, and continued in office till his death in 1646*. Many curious and magnificent

---

* That lodges continued regularly to assemble at this time, appears from the diary of the learned antiquary Elias Ashmole, where he says, ' I was ' made a free-mason at Warrington, Lancashire, ' with Colonel Henry Mainwaring, of Kerthingham, ' in Cheshire, by Mr. Richard Penket the Warden, ' and the fellow-crafts (all of whom are specified) on
' 16th

nificent structures were finished under the direction of this accomplished architect,

'16th October 1646.' In another place of his diary he says, 'On March the 10th 1682, about 5 hor.
'post merid. I received a summons to appear at a
'lodge to be held the next day at masons' hall in
'London.—March 11, Accordingly I went, and
'about noon were admitted into the fellowship of
'free-masons Sir William Wilson, Kt. Capt. Richard
'Borthwick, Mr. William Woodman, Mr. William
'Gray, Mr. Samuel Taylour, and Mr. William
'Wise. I was the senior fellow among them, it be-
'ing thirty five years since I was admitted. There
'were present, beside myself, the fellows after-
'named; Mr. Thomas Wise, master of the masons'
'company this present year, Mr. Thomas Shorthose,
'and 7 more old free masons. We all dined at the
'Half-Moon tavern, Cheapside, at a noble dinner
'prepared at the charge of the new accepted ma-
'sons.'

An old record of the society describes a coat of arms much the same with that of the London company of freemen masons; whence it is generally believed that this company is descended of that ancient fraternity; and in former times, no man, it also appears, was made free of that company until he was initiated in some lodge of free and accepted masons, as a necessary qualification. This practice still prevails in Scotland among the operative masons.

and

and among the rest that noble edifice the Banqueting house at Whitehall, the foundation-stone of which was laid in the year 1607 in the royal presence.

The breaking out of the civil wars obstructed the progress of Masonry in England for some time; after the Restoration, however, it began to revive under the patronage of Charles II. who had been received into the Order while on his travels. On the 27th December 1663, a general assembly was held, at which Henry Jermyn, earl of St. Alban's, was elected Grand Master, who appointed Sir John Denham, Kt. his deputy, and Mr. (afterwards Sir) Christopher Wren, and John Webb his wardens. Several regulations * were

---

* Among other regulations that were made at this assembly, were the following:

'1. That no person, of what degree soever, be
' made or accepted a free-mason unless in a regular
' lodge, whereof one to be a Master or a Warden
' in that limit or division where such lodge is kept,
' and another to be a craftsman in the trade of Free-
' masonry.

'2. That

were made at this assembly, and the greatest harmony prevailed among the fraternity.

Thomas

'2. That no person hereafter shall be accepted a
'free-mason, but such as are of able body, honest
'parentage, good reputation, and an observer of
'the laws of the land.

'3. That no person hereafter who shall be ac-
'cepted a free-mason shall be admitted into any
'lodge or assembly, until he has brought a certifi-
'cate of the time and place of his acceptation from
'the lodge that accepted him, unto the master of
'that limit or division where such lodge is kept:
'And the said Master shall enrol the same in a roll
'of parchment to be kept for that purpose, and
'shall give an account of all such acceptations at
'every general assembly.

'4. That every person who is now a free-mason
'shall bring to the Master a note of the time of his
'acceptation, to the end the same may be enrolled
'in such priority of place as the brother deserves;
'and that the whole company and fellows may the
'better know each other.

'5. That for the future the said fraternity of
'free-masons shall be regulated and governed by
'one Grand Master, and as many Wardens as the
'said society shall think fit to appoint at every an-
'nual general assembly.

'6. That no person shall be accepted, unless he
'be twenty-one years old, or more.'

Many

OF MASONRY. 241

Thomas Savage, earl of Rivers, succeeding the earl of St. Albans in the office of Grand Master in June 1666, Sir Christopher Wren was appointed Deputy under his Lordship. No Grand Officer ever distinguished himself more than Sir Christopher Wren, in promoting the prosperity of the few lodges, which occasionally met at this time. The honours which he afterwards received in the Society are evident proofs of the attachment the fraternity bore to him.

Sir Christopher Wren was the only son of Dr. Christopher Wren, dean of Windsor, and was born in 1632. His genius for the arts and sciences appeared early. At the age of thirteen he invented a new astronomical instrument, by the name of Pan-organum, and wrote a treatise on the origin of rivers. He invented a pneumatic engine, and a

---

Many of the fraternity's records of this and the preceding reigns were lost at the Revolution; and not a few were too hastily burnt in our own times by some scrupulous brothers, from a fear of making discoveries prejudicial to the interest of Masonry.

peculiar instrument of use in gnomonics to solve this problem: 'On a known 'plane, in a known elevation, to describe 'such lines with the expedite turning of 'rundles to certain divisions, as by the 'shadow of the stile may shew the equal 'hours of the day.' In 1646, he was admitted a gentleman-commoner in Wadham College Oxon, where he greatly improved under the instructions and friendship of Dr. John Wilkins, and Dr. Seth Ward. His juvenile productions in mathematics prove him both a scholar and a genius. His studies were not confined. He assisted Dr. Scarborough in the anatomical preparations and experiments upon the muscles of the human body, and wrote several discourses on the longitude, navigation, &c.

After the fire of London, Sir Christopher was appointed principal architect for rebuilding the city. By his Majesty's command he drew up a plan for that purpose, which was much approved; but private property interfering, it was not adopted.

adopted. The city, however, was rebuilt in a much better style than before.

On the 23d of October 1667, the King in person laid the foundation stone of the Royal Exchange, which was opened in September following. In 1673, his Majesty also laid the foundation stone of St. Paul's, in presence of the Grand Master and his officers, the lord mayor and aldermen, the bishops and clergy, and several of the nobility and gentry, amidst the acclamations of a number of spectators. This superb structure was begun, carried on, and finished by the fraternity, under the direction of Sir Christopher, after his own design; as were also Chelsea-hospital and Greenwich palace.

Several lodges were constituted about this time, and the best architects resorted to them. In 1674 the earl of Rivers having resigned, George Villiers, duke of Buckingham, was elected Grand Master. He left the care of the masons to his wardens and Sir Christopher, who still continued to act as deputy. In 1679 the duke refigned in favour of Henry Bennett, earl of Arlington; but he being too deeply engaged in ftate affairs, neglected to attend the duties of the office; the lodges, however, continued to affemble under his fanction, and many worthy and refpectable gentlemen joined them.

On the death of the King in 1685, James II. fucceeded to the throne; but the fraternity were much neglected in his reign. The earl of Arlington dying this year, the lodges met in communication, and elected Sir Chriftopher Wren Grand Mafter. He appointed Mr. Gabriel Cibber, and Mr. Edward Strong, his wardens. Though Mafonry had been in a declining ftate for many years, feveral lodges were now occafionally held in different places.

At the Revolution, Mafonry was fo much reduced, that there were no more than feven regular lodges in London and its fuburbs, of which two only are worthy of notice; the old lodge of St. Paul's, over which Sir Chriftopher prefided, during the building of that ftructure; and a lodge

lodge at St. Thomas's hospital, Southwark, over which Sir Robert Clayton, then lord mayor of London, presided, during the rebuilding of that hospital.

In 1695 King William was privately initiated into the Order. His Majesty approved of the brethren's choice of Sir Christopher Wren, and patronized the lodges; particularly one at Hampton Court, which was held during the building the new part of that palace. Kensington palace was built, and Chelsea hospital finished by the fraternity under the auspices of Sir Christopher Wren. The palace of Greenwich also, being converted, at this time, into an hospital for seamen, his Majesty ordered to be finished after the design of Inigo Jones.

In 1697 a general assembly and feast of the free-masons was held, at which many noble and eminent brethren attended. Charles duke of Richmond and Lenox, master of a lodge at Chichester, being present at this feast, was proposed Grand Master for the following year, and unanimously elected.

elected. He engaged Sir Christopher Wren to act as his deputy, and appointed Edward Strong senior, and Edward Strong junior, his wardens. Next year Sir Christopher was elected his successor, and the fraternity continued to assemble under the patronage of this architect, till he died in 1702.

In the following reign Masonry was at a low ebb, Sir Christopher's age and infirmities withdrawing his attention from the lodges, they gradually decreased, and the annual festivals were entirely neglected. The old lodge at St. Paul's, and a few others, continued to meet, but these consisted of few members. It was therefore resolved that the privileges of Masonry should no longer be limited to architects and operative masons, but that men of different professions might be admitted, who should agree to support the dignity of the Order as an ancient and respectable society.

On the accession of George I. the lodges resolved to cement under a new Grand Master,

Master, to be annually elected as in former times, to revive the communications and festivals of the Society, to regulate the ancient usages and customs of the fraternity, and to establish such modes only as might correspond with the practices of the members of which the lodges were now principally composed. Accordingly, on the festival of St. John the Baptist, in 1717, a general assembly of the fraternity was convened. Four lodges attended in form, and a grand lodge was constituted. The oldest mason present being in the chair, the brethren proceeded to elect a Grand Master for the ensuing year, when the choice fell upon Anthony Sayer, gent. who was declared duly elected. Mr. Sayer was succeeded in 1718, by George Payne, Esq. This gentleman was particularly attentive to the duties of his office; he carefully collected many old papers and manuscripts relating to Masonry, of which several were afterwards digested, and properly arranged by Dr. James Anderson in a book,

book, entitled, 'The Constitutions of the Ancient and Honourable Society of Free and Accepted Masons.' From this era we may date the revival of Masonry in England, the lodges daily increasing, both in the quantity and quality of their members, under the mild and careful administration of Mr. Payne. This gentleman continued to preside over the fraternity till the year 1721, when he was succeeded by the duke of Montagu.

The Duke was installed on the 24th of June at Stationers' hall, in the presence of a numerous company of masons. Lord Stanhope, afterwards earl of Chesterfield, was initiated into Masonry on the morning of the same day, at an occasional lodge held at the Queen's Arms tavern in St. Paul's church-yard. Several respectable gentlemen were introduced into the Society at the same time, and great harmony prevailed among the fraternity.

The Grand Master, soon after his election, gave convincing proofs of his zeal for Masonry. He commanded Dr. Desaguliers faguliers and James Anderſon, A. M. both men of genius and education, to arrange and digeſt the Gothic conſtitutions, and reviſe the old charges. This taſk they faithfully executed, and in little more than two years the Book of Conſtitutions appeared in print.

Maſonry now flouriſhed, and ſeveral lodges were conſtituted. The communications were regularly convened, and the Grand Maſter's conſtant attendance gave a ſanction to all the proceedings.

In 1722, his Grace reſigned in favour of the duke of Wharton, who was very ambitious of the office. This reſignation proceeded from a deſire of reconciling the brethren to that nobleman, as he had incurred their diſpleaſure by convening an irregular aſſembly of maſons at Stationers" hall on the feſtival of St. John the Baptiſt, by whom he had been elected Grand Maſter in oppoſition to the reſolutions of the Grand Lodge. His Grace having publicly acknowledged his error, and promiſed in future to conform to the laws, was regularly inſtalled,

installed, and congratulated by upwards of twenty-five lodges. His activity and vigilance in office, and his attention to the lodges, soon recovered the good opinion of the brethren. During his presidency, the office of Grand Secretary was established, and William Cowper Esq; continued to execute the duty of that department for several years.

The duke of Buccleugh succeeded the duke of Wharton in June 1723. This nobleman was no less attached to Masonry than his predecessor. Being absent on the annual festival, he was installed by proxy at Merchant-taylors hall, in presence of 400 masons.

His Grace was succeeded, in the year following, by the duke of Richmond, under whose administration the Committee of Charity was instituted*. Lord Paisley, afterwards

---

* The duke of Buccleugh first proposed the scheme of raising a general fund for distressed masons. Lord Paisley, Dr. Desaguliers, Colonel Houghton, and a few other brethren, supported the Duke's proposition. The Grand Lodge appointed a committee to consider

wards earl of Abercorn, being active in promoting this new establishment, was elected Grand Master at the end of the year 1725. Being

consider of the most effectual means of carrying the scheme into execution. The report of the committee was transmitted to the lodges, and afterwards approved by the Grand Lodge. The disposal of the charity was at first vested in seven brethren, but this number being found too small, nine more were added. It was afterwards resolved, that twelve masters of contributing lodges, in rotation, with the Grand Officers, should form the committee; and by another regulation since made, it has been determined, that all past and present Grand Officers, with the Masters of all regular lodges which shall have contributed within twelve months to the charity, shall be members of the committee: which regulation is still in force.

The committee meet three times in the year by virtue of a summons from the Grand Master or his Deputy. The petitions of the brethren, who apply for charity, are considered at these meetings; and if the petitioner is found to be a deserving object, he is immediately relieved with five pounds: if the circumstances of his case are of a singular nature, as being reduced by some unexpected misfortune from a state of affluence to poverty, or being burdened with a numerous family, and incapable of providing for them, his petition is referred to the next communication, where he is relieved

Being in the country at the time, his Lordship was inſtalled by proxy. During his abſence, Dr. Deſaguliers, who had been appointed his deputy, was very attentive to the duties of the office; he viſited the lodges, and diligently promoted Maſonry. On his Lordſhip's return to town, the earl of Inchiquin was propoſed to ſucceed him, and was elected in February

with any ſum the Committee may have ſpecified, not exceeding twenty guineas at one time. By this means the diſtreſſed have always found ready relief from this general charity, which is ſolely ſupported by the voluntary contributions of the different lodges out of their private fund, without being burdenſome on any member of the ſociety.

Thus the Committee of Charity has been eſtabliſhed among the Free and Accepted Maſons of England; and though the ſums annually expended to relieve diſtreſſed brethren, have, for ſeveral years paſt, amounted to many hundred pounds, there ſtill remains (A. D. 1774) undiſtributed 1500l. in the three per cent. bank annuities conſolidated, and one hundred pound, and upwards in the hands of the Grand Treaſurer.

All complaints and informations are conſidered at the Committee of Charity, and from thence a report is made to the Grand Lodge, where it is generally approved.

1726.

1726. The society flourished, at this time, both in town and country, and, under the auspices of this nobleman, the office of Provincial Grand Master * was established, and the first deputation granted for Wales. His Lordship was succeeded in December by Lord Coleraine, who constituted several lodges, and among the rest, one at Madrid. Several new regulations were made during his administration, particularly one concerning the Stewards, which office was now revived, and their number restricted to twelve annually.

Lord Kingston succeeded Lord Coleraine in December 1728, who also proved a zealous friend to the Society. As a

---

* A Provincial Grand Master is invested with the power and honour of a Deputy Grand Master, and is authorized to constitute lodges within his province. He is intitled to wear the clothing of a Grand Officer, and ranks in all public assemblies immediately after the Past Deputy Grand Masters. He is enjoined to correspond with the Grand Lodge, and to transmit a circumstantial account of his proceedings to the Grand Secretary at least once in every year.

testimony

testimony of his regard, he presented to the Grand Lodge a curious pedestal, and a rich cushion with gold knobs and fringes; a velvet bag, and a fine jewel set in gold, for the use of the Secretary. During his Lordship's administration a deputation was granted to constitute a lodge at Bengal, over which George Pomfret Esq; was appointed to preside. This proved a favourable introduction to Masonry in that quarter of the world. Upwards of fifty lodges have been since constituted in the East Indies, of which eleven are now held at Bengal.

The duke of Norfolk was the next patron of the Society. He was elected Grand Master in the beginning of the year 1730. His Grace was vigilant in office, and when his private affairs called him into Italy, was not unmindful of the fraternity. He transmitted the following noble presents from Venice; viz. twenty pounds to the charity; a large folio book of the finest writing paper for the records of the Grand Lodge, richly bound

bound in turkey and gilt, with a curious frontispiece in vellum, containing the arms of Norfolk, amply displayed, with a Latin inscription of the family titles, and the arms of Masonry; and the old trusty sword of Gustavus Adolphus, King of Sweden, (that was next wore by his successor in war, the brave Bernard, duke of Saxe-Weimar, with both their names on the blade, and further enriched with the arms of Norfolk in silver on the scabbard) to be the Grand Master's sword of state. Lodges were constituted both in Germany and America under his Grace's patronage.

Lord Lovel, afterwards earl of Leicester, succeeded the duke of Norfolk in the office of Grand Master, and was installed at Mercers' Hall in March 1731. During his Lordship's presidency, a deputation was sent to the Hague to form a lodge there for the initiation of his late Imperial Majesty, who was soon after advanced to the degree of a master-mason in England. This event the Society have in continual remembrance.

In April 1732, Lord Viscount Montacute was elected Grand Master. In the course of his mastership one lodge was constituted in Paris, and another at Valenciennes in French Flanders.

The earl of Strathmore succeeded lord Montacute in June 1733. His Lordship granted a deputation to eleven German masons to constitute a lodge at Hamburgh, and during his presidency the society was in a very flourishing state. Several genteel presents were now received from the East Indies.

The earl of Crawford being elected Grand Master in March 1734, and public affairs attracting his attention, the communications of the Grand Lodge were neglected almost a whole year; to atone for this omission, however, two were held in the space of six weeks. His Lordship ordered brother James Anderson to prepare the Book of Constitutions for a second edition. This diligent scholar accordingly obeyed the command, and a new edition was produced in print in January 1738, much improved and greatly enlarged.

enlarged. The Stewards, about this time, applied to the Grand Lodge for certain privileges, which were granted them.

Lord Weymouth succeeded the earl of Crawford in April 1735. During his presidency several lodges were constituted, and, among the rest, the Stewards' lodge. In consequence of a resolution of the Society this year, the Stewards sent twelve representatives to the Grand Lodge, who appeared there in their regalia, for the first time, in December, but were not permitted to vote.

The earl of Loudon succeeded lord Weymouth in April 1736, and under his Lordship a lodge was constituted in Africa. Next year the earl of Darnley was elected Grand Master, in whose administration Frederick, late prince of Wales, father of his present Majesty, was initiated, at an occasional lodge held at Kew, over which Dr. Desaguliers presided. The Earl appointed several Provincial Grand Masters for foreign parts.

The marquis of Carnarvon, afterwards duke of Chandois, was elected Grand

Master in April 1738. About this time a scheme was proposed for placing out the sons of masons   , but, after long debates   was rejected. His Grac   ..ted the Society with a large   ld for the use of the Secretary,   wo cross pens in a L   knots   points of the pens b   most curiously enamelled.

Lord Raymond succeeded the marquis of Carnar   in May 17 9 His Lordship, in several communications, redressed many grievances complained of, and ordered the laws to be strictly enforced against some lodges, on account of irregularities which then prevailed*. Several lodges were constituted by his Lordship.

The

---

* Several persons, disgusted at some of the proceedings of the Grand Lodge at this time, renounced their allegiance to the Grand Master, and, in opposition to the original laws of the Society, and their solemn ties, held meetings, made masons, and, falsely assuming the appellation of a Grand Lodge, even presumed to constitute lodges. The regular masons, finding it necessary to check their progress, adopted some new measures. Piqued at this proceeding, they endeavoured to propagate an opinion,

The earl of Kintore succeeded lord Raymond in April 1740, and, in imitation of his predecessor, continued to discourage all irregularities. His Lordship appointed several Provincials, in particular one for Russia, another for Hamburgh and the circle of Lower Saxony, and another for the island of Barbadoes.

The earl of Morton was elected on the 19th of March following, and installed the same day, with great solemnity, in the presence of a very respectable company of nobility, foreign ambassadors, and others. Several seasonable laws were passed during his Lordship's mastership, and some regulations made concerning processions and other ceremonies. His Lordship presented a staff of office to the Treasurer of neat workmanship, and the

opinion, that the ancient practices of the Society were retained by them, and totally abolished by the regular lodges, on whom they conferred the appellation of *Modern Masons*. By this artifice they continued to impose on the public, and introduced several gentlemen into their assemblies; but of late years, the fallacy being detected, they have not been so successful.

Grand

Grand Lodge resolved that the Treasurer should be annually elected, and, with the Secretary and Sword-bearer, be members of the Grand Lodge. A large cornelian seal, with the arms of Masonry, set in gold, was presented to the Society, at this time, by brother Vaughan, his Lordship's Senior Warden.

Lord Ward succeeded the earl of Morton in April 1742. His Lordship was well acquainted with the nature and government of the Society, having served every office, even from a Secretary in a private lodge. His Lordship lost no time in applying the most effectual remedies to reconcile all animosities; he recommended to his officers the greatest vigilance and care in their different departments; and, by his own conduct, set them a noble example how to support the dignity of the Society. Many lodges which were in a declining state, he advised to coalesce with others in the like circumstances; some who had been negligent in their attendance on the communications, after proper admonitions, he
restored

restored to favour; and others, who persevered in their contumacy, he erased out of the list. Thus his Lordship manifested the most tender regard for the interest of the Society, while his lenity and forbearance were universally esteemed. The unanimity and harmony of the lodges never shone more conspicuous than under his Lordship's administration. He appointed several Provincial Grand Masters, and constituted many lodges both at home and abroad. The free-masons at Antigua, having built a large hall in that island for their meetings, applied to the Grand Lodge for liberty to be styled the Great Lodge of St. John's in Antigua: This favour was granted in April 1744. His Lordship continued two years at the head of the fraternity, and was succeeded by the earl of Strathmore, during whose administration, being chiefly absent the whole time, the care and management of the Society devolved on the other Grand Officers, who were very active for the general good of the fraternity. His Lordship appointed a Provincial Grand Master for the island of Bermudas.

Lord

Lord Cranstoun was elected Grand Master in April 1745, and presided over the fraternity, with great reputation, two years. Under his auspices Masonry flourished, and several new lodges were constituted. By a resolution of the Grand Lodge, at this time, it was ordered, that public processions on feast-days should be discontinued. This resolution was occasioned by some mock processions, which a few disgusted brethren had formed, in order to ridicule these public appearances.

Lord Byron succeeded lord Cranstoun, and was installed at Drapers'-hall on the 30th of April 1747. The laws of the committee of charity were, by his Lordship's orders, inspected, printed, and distributed among the lodges. A handsome contribution to the General Charity was sent from the lodge at Gibraltar. During five years that his Lordship presided over the fraternity, no diligence was spared, on his part, to preserve the privileges of Masonry, to redress grievances, and to relieve distress. When business required his attendance in the country, Fotherley Baker Esq; the Deputy Grand Master, and Secretary Revis were particularly attentive to the Society in his absence. The first gentleman was distinguished for his knowledge of the laws and regulations; the latter for his long and faithful services. Under the direction of these gentlemen the Society continued till the year 1752, when lord Carysfort accepted the office of Grand Master. The influence of his Lordship's application to the real interests of the fraternity soon became visible to all, and the public fund was considerably increased. No Grand Officer ever took more pains to preserve, or was more attentive to recommend, order and decorum. He was ready, on all occasions, to visit the lodges in person, and to promote harmony among the members. Dr. Manningham, his Deputy, was no less vigilant in the execution of his duty. He constantly visited the lodges in his Lordship's absence, and used his best endeavours to cement union among the brethren. The whole proceedings of this

active

active officer were conducted with great prudence, and his candor and affability gained him univerſal reſpect. The Grand Maſter's attachment to the Society was no leſs conſpicuous. Under his Lordſhip's patronage the lodges flouriſhed, and much harmony reigned among them. The brethren, as a teſtimony of their ſenſe of his Lordſhip's great ſervices, re-elected him Grand Maſter on the 3d of April 1753.

The Marquis of Carnarvon (now Duke of Chandois) ſucceeded lord Caryſfort. He began his adminiſtration by ordering the Book of Conſtitutions to be reprinted, under the inſpection of the Reverend Dr. Entick. His zeal for Maſonry, and his attention to the intereſts of the ſociety, were alike conſpicuous. He continued to preſide over the fraternity till the year 1757, when he reſigned in favour of lord Aberdour; during whoſe adminiſtration the Grand Lodge took into conſideration a complaint againſt certain brethren for forming and aſſembling under the falſe denomination of ancient maſons, who, as ſuch, conſidered themſelves independent

of

of the society, and not subject to the laws of the Grand Lodge, or to the control of the Grand Master. Dr. Manningham, the Deputy Grand Master, pointed out the necessity of discouraging all such meetings, as they were not only contrary to the original laws of the society, but an open violation of the allegiance due to the Grand Master. He likewise observed, that they tended to introduce into the craft the novelties and conceits of opinionative persons, and raise a belief that there have been other societies of masons more ancient than that of this ancient and honourable Society. Upon which the Grand Lodge resolved, that the meeting of any brethren of this society, under any denomination of masons, without a legal power or authority granted by the Grand Master for the time being, is inconsistent with the honour and interest of Masonry, and an open violation of the established laws of the Order. Fourteen persons were, soon after, expelled the society, for countenancing these irregular assemblies. Lord Aberdour held the office of Grand

Master till 1762, when earl Ferrers was elected, during whose presidency nothing remarkable occurred.

Lord Blaney succeeded earl Ferrers in 1764. His Lordship continued in office two years, during which time, being chiefly in Ireland, the business of the society was faithfully executed by his Deputy Col. Salter, an active and vigilant officer. Their Royal Highnesses the Dukes of Gloucester and Cumberland were initiated into the Order during the presidency of lord Blaney.

The duke of Beaufort succeeded his Lordship in 1767, and governed the Society with honour and reputation five years. A scheme being proposed in 1768 to incorporate the society, and to raise a fund to build a hall * and purchase furniture,

---

* It is greatly to be lamented, that the society of masons, so numerous, and so highly honoured in its members, (being in a great degree composed of persons of rank and fortune) should, as oft as they have occasion for general meetings, be obliged to resort to taverns, or to hire halls of other communities, and those, at the best, but ill adapted

ture, &c. for the Grand Lodge, his Grace generously contributed to the design, and, though opposed by a few brethren who misconceived his good intentions, strenuously persevered in promoting every measure for the purpose. Our meeting at the houses of publicans, gives us the air of a Bacchanalian society; instead of that appearance of gravity and dignity, which the Order requires. For masons, united under the serious regulations of morality and philosophy, to associate in taverns, the receptacles of revelry and licentiousness, must appear, even on the first view, to be ridiculous and absurd!

The necessity of a hall for our general meetings is universally acknowledged through the society; and a desire of seeing one erected, as generally prevails.—How afflicting must it be to the worthy mason, daily to receive accounts from travelling brethren, of the magnificence of the lodges abroad; while the Grand Lodge of England, which, in many respects is intitled to a preference in dignity to all others, is destitute of a building, which they can call their own. But, not to rest on general accounts, we shall here give a particular description of the Banquetting Hall belonging to the lodge of St. John at Marseilles; and from the magnificence and splendor of that room, to which the brethren only retire for refreshment, there may be formed some idea of the superior excellence which ought to distinguish the lodge room.

sure that might facilitate its execution. A bill was brought into parliament in 1771,

At the bottom of the hall, under a gilded canopy, the valences whereof are blue, fringed with gold, is a painting, which represents the genius of Masonry supporting the portrait of the King of France, upon a pedestal, with this inscription:

Dilectissimo Regi Monumentum
Amoris
Latomi,   Massilienses.

[The MASONS at Marseilles have erected this monument of their affection to their most beloved King.]

A genius seated below the pedestal, presents with one hand this inscription, and with the other the arms of the lodge, with their motto:

Deo, Regi, et Patriæ, Fidelitas.

[Fidelity to God, our King, and Country.]

Above this is a genius which crowns the King.

To the right of this painting is placed another, representing the wisdom of SOLOMON, with this inscription above it,—*Prudentia.* [Prudence.]

To the left is another, representing the courage of St. John the Baptist, in remonstrating with HEROD upon his debaucheries. The inscription above it is,—*Fortitudo.* [Fortitude.]

The right side of the hall is ornamented with paintings of equal grandeur.

The first represents JOSEPH acknowledging his brethren, and pardoning them for the ill usage he had received from them, with this inscription,—*Venia.* [Pardon.]

The

1771, by the Hon. Charles Dillon then Deputy Grand Mafter, to obtain a charter
of

The fecond reprefents JOB upon the dunghill, his houfe deftroyed, his fields laid wafte by ftorm, his wife infulting him, and himfelf calm, lifting his hands towards heaven, with this infcription,—*Patientia.* [Patience.]

The third reprefents St. PAUL and St. BARNABAS, refufing divine honours at Lyftra, with this infcription,—*Humilitas.* [Humility.]

The fourth, JONATHAN, when he warned DAVID to keep from the city, in order to avoid the danger which threatened his days, with this infcription,—*Amicitia.* [Friendfhip.]

The fifth, SOLOMON furveying the works of the Temple, and giving his orders for the execution of the plan, which his father DAVID had left him of it, with this infcription,—*Pietas.* [Piety.]

The fixth, the charity of the SAMARITAN, with this infcription,—*Charitas.* [Charity.]

The feventh, St. PETER and the other apoftles paying tribute to CÆSAR, by means of the piece of money found miraculoufly in the belly of a fifh, with this infcription,—*Fidelitas.* [Fidelity.]

The left fide of the hall contains three paintings.

The firft, TOBIAS curing his father, with thefe words for the infcription,—*Filiale Debitum.* [Filial Debt.]

The fecond, the father of the prodigal fon, when

of incorporation for the Society, which was twice read in the House of Commons, but

he embraces him, and pardons his offences. with this inscription,—*Paternus Amor.* [Paternal Love.]

The third represents the sacrifice of ABRAHAM, with this inscription,—*Obedientia.* [Obedience.]

On each side the door are two paintings of equal grandeur.

One represents the apostles giving alms in common; the inscription,—*Eleemosyna.* [Alms-giving.]

The other represents LOT, receiving the angels into his house, believing them to be strangers; the inscription is,—*Hospitalitas.* [Hospitality.]

The four corners of the hall are decorated with four allegorical pictures.

In one are represented two geniuses holding a large medal, in which are painted three pillars of a gold colour, with this motto,

Hic posuere locum, Virtus, Sapientia, Forma.
[Here Virtue, Wisdom, Beauty, fixed their seat.]

In another, two geniuses equally supporting a large medal, on which are represented three hearts set on fire by the same flame, united by the bond of the Order, with this motto,

Pectora jungit Amor, Pietasque ligavit Amantes.
[Love joins their hearts, and Piety the tie.]

The two others are in the same taste, but supported by one genius only, being a smaller size. The medals represent as follows:

The

but being opposed by Mr. Onslow, at the desire of several of the brethren themselves,

The first, three branches; one of olive, another of laurel, and another of myrtle; with this motto,
Hic Pacem mutuo damus, accipimusque vicissim.
[Here Peace we give, and here by turns receive.]
The other a level in a hand coming from heaven, placed perpendicularly upon a heap of stones of unequal forms and sizes, with this motto,
Equa Lege sortitur Insignes et Imos.
[One equal Law, of high and low the lot.]
All these paintings are upon a line; those which are placed opposite the windows are intirely in front. Over the inner door of entrance is this inscription, in a painting which is displayed by a child,
S. T. O. T. A.
Varia hæc Virtutum Exempla Fraternæ Liberalitatis Monumenta D. V. & C. Latomi Massilienses, Fratribus quæ assequenda præbent, anno Lucis 5765.
The letters S. T. O. T. A. signify,
Supremo Totius Orbis Terrarum Architecto.
[The master, vice-master, and whole body of the masons at Marseilles have erected these different examples of the virtues and monuments of fraternal liberality, proposed to the imitation of their brethren, to the honour of the supreme architect of the whole world; in the year of light 5765.]

Each painting bears below-it, the arms and blazon of the brethren who caused them to be painted.

felves, who had petitioned the Houfe againſt it, Mr. Dillon moved to poſtpone the

Every ſpace, from one column to another, forms an intercolumniation. Upon the middle of each pilaſter, being twenty-four in number, are raiſed corbals, in form of antique Guaines, upon which are placed the buſts of the great and virtuous men of antiquity.

The curtains to the gilded canopy are in the Italian taſte, and are four in number.

Three great branches of chryſtal, light this hall at proper times, and ſerve as additional ornaments.

The above deſcription does not exceed the ſplendor of many other lodges in foreign countries. In Ruſſia, Holland, and ſeveral parts of Germany, according to the accounts we have received, the lodges even ſurpaſs this in elegance; particularly one in Berlin, under the King of Pruſſia, our royal brother. Theſe are hung with the richeſt velvets, tapeſtries, embroideries, and gold lace; and are ornamented with every coſtly luſtre and ſuitable decoration. The illuminated brilliancy theſe make, added to the polite order and harmony of the members, and the grandeur of the muſic, confiſting of ſeveral different bands, ſtrike a moſt grateful and pleaſing concord, while they fill the mind of every brother with the idea of a heavenly manſion, and the pleaſures of an angelic aſſociation †.

† Edmondes' Addreſs to the Free Maſons.

the confideration of the bill *fine die*. Thus this grand defign fell to the ground. The fcheme for building a hall, however, is ftill in agitation, ground having been purchafed for that purpofe, and upwards of 1500 l. already fubfcribed.

The duke of Beaufort was fucceeded by lord Petre, the prefent Grand Mafter,

It is therefore greatly to be wifhed that the brethren of this kingdom, the grand center of Mafonry, could be induced to extend their generofity; and, by embracing the opportunity, while princes of the blood are our patrons, and noblemen of the moft diftinguifhed virtue are our rulers, immediately to promote a voluntary contribution for erecting, in this country, a fuperb and magnificent ftructure for the general affemblies of the fraternity; that it might be recorded, to the honour of the prefent age, that every encouragement was given to a fociety, whofe chief purfuit is the acquifition of knowledge, and the cultivation of virtue.

Such a fcheme is now in agitation, and every zealous friend to the caufe ought to exert his influence on the occafion, and not let it fall to the ground for want of fupport. Though the fums we have received are as yet inconfiderable, if we perfevere with fpirit in the profecution of our laudable defign, there is little doubt but we fhall happily fucceed in our greateft expectations.

a nobleman

a nobleman of exemplary character in private life, and equally zealous, with his predeceffor, in promoting the profperity of the craft. Under his Lordfhip's aufpices the Society daily increafes, and the fcience of Mafonry is diligently propagated, both at home and abroad.

Having brought down the hiftory of Mafonry in England to the prefent time, I fhall conclude with obferving, that the Society now flourifhes, in almoft every part of the known world, under the patronage of men of the firft rank and character.

A COLLECTION

OF

Odes, Anthems, and Songs.

ODE I.

HAIL to the CRAFT! at whose serene command,
  The gentle ARTS in glad obedience stand:
Hail, sacred MASONRY! of source divine,
Unerring sov'reign of th' unerring line:
Whose plumb of truth, with never failing sway,
Makes the join'd parts of symmetry obey:
Whose magic stroke bids fell confusion cease,
And to the finish'd ORDERS gives a place:
Who rears vast structures from the womb of earth,
And gives imperial cities glorious birth.
  To works of Art HER merit not confin'd,
SHE regulates the morals, squares the mind;
Corrects with care the sallies of the soul,
And points the tide of passions where to roll:
On virtue's tablet marks HER moral rule,
And forms her Lodge an universal school;

Where

ADVERTISEMENT.

IN the First Edition no Songs were inserted but those that were sung at the Gala: As the description of that performance is now omitted, we have thought it unnecessary to limit our collection to the Songs used on that occasion; we have therefore added several others which are usually sung in the course of the ceremonies explained in this Work.

A
COLLECTION
OF
Odes, Anthems, and Songs
ON
MASONRY.

Where Nature's myſtic laws unfolded ſtand,
And Senſe and Science join'd, go hand in hand.
  O may HER ſocial rules inſtructive ſpread,
Till Truth erect HER long neglected head!
Till thro' deceitful night SHE dart HER ray,
And beam full glorious in the blaze of day!
Till men by virtuous maxims learn to move,
Till all the peopled world HER laws approve,
And Adam's race are bound in brothers' love.

ODE II.

WAKE the lute and quiv'ring ſtrings,
Myſtic truths Urania brings;
Friendly viſitant, to thee,
We owe the depths of MASONRY:
Faireſt of the virgin choir,
Warbling to the golden lyre,
Welcome, here thy ART prevail:
Hail! divine Urania, hail!

Here, in Friendſhip's ſacred bower,
The downy wing'd, and ſmiling hour,
Mirth invites, and ſocial ſong,
Nameleſs myſteries among:
Crown the bowl and fill the glaſs,
To every virtue, every grace,
To the BROTHERHOOD reſound
Health, and let it thrice go round.

We reſtore the times of old,
The blooming glorious age of gold;
As the new creation free,
Bleſt with gay Euphroſyne;

We with god-like Science talk,
And with fair Astrea walk;
Innocence adorns the day,
Brighter than the smiles of May.

Pour the rosy wine again,
Wake a louder, louder strain;
Rapid Zephyrs, as ye fly,
Waft our voices to the sky;
While we celebrate the NINE,
And the wonders of the Trine,
While the ANGELS sing above,
As we below, of PEACE and LOVE.

ANTHEM I.

GRANT us, kind Heav'n, what we request,
In Masonry let us be blest;
Direct us to that happy place
Where Friendship smiles in every face:
    Where Freedom and sweet Innocence
    Enlarge the mind and cheer the sense.

Where scepter'd Reason, from her throne,
Surveys the LODGE, and makes us one;
And Harmony's delightful sway
For ever sheds ambrosial day;
    Where we blest Eden's pleasure taste,
    Whilst balmy joys are our repast.

No prying eye can view us here;
No fool or knave disturb our cheer:
Our well form'd laws set mankind free,
And give relief to Misery:
    The Poor, oppressed with woe and grief,
    Gain from our bounteous hands relief.

Our LODGE the social Virtues grace,
And Wisdom's rules we fondly trace;
Whole Nature, open to our view,
Points out the paths we shou!d pursue.
    Let us subsist in lasting peace,
    And may our happiness increase.

ANTHEM II.

BY Masons' Art th' aspiring dome
    On stately columns shall arise,
All climates are their native home,
    Their godlike actions reach the skies.
Heroes and Kings revere their name,
While Poets sing their lasting fame.

    Great, noble, gen'rous, good, and brave;
        All virtues they most justly claim;
    Their deeds shall live beyond the grave,
        And those unborn their praise proclaim.
Time shall their glorious acts enrol,
While love and friendship charm the soul.

SONG I.

[*Tune*, Attic Fire.]

ARISE, and blow thy trumpet, Fame!
Free-Masonry aloud proclaim,
    To realms and worlds unknown:
Tell them of mighty David's son,
The wise, the matchless Solomon,
    Priz'd far above his throne.

The solemn temple's cloud-capt towers,
Th' aspiring domes are works of ours,
    By us those piles were rais'd:
Then bid mankind with songs advance,
And through th' ethereal vast expanse,
    Let Masonry be prais'd.

We help the poor in time of need,
The naked clothe, the hungry feed,
    'Tis our foundation stone:
We build upon the noblest plan;
For friendship rivets man to man, } *Chorus 3 times.*
    And makes us all as one.

Still louder, Fame, thy trumpet blow;
Let all the distant regions know
    Free-Masonry is this.
Almighty Wisdom gave it birth,
And Heav'n has fix'd it here on earth,
    A type of future bliss.

SONG II.

[*Tune*, He comes, &c.]

UNITE, unite, your voices raise;
Loud, loudly sing Free-Masons' praise:
Spread far and wide their spotless fame,
And glory in the sacred name.

Behold, behold, the upright band,
In virtue's paths go hand in hand;
They shun each ill, they do no wrong,
Strict honour does to them belong.

How juſt, how juſt, are all their ways,
Superior far to mortal praiſe ;
Their worth deſcription far exceeds,
For matchleſs are Free-Maſons' deeds.

Go on, go on, ye juſt and true,
Still, ſtill the ſame bright paths purſue ;
Th' admiring world ſhall on ye gaze,
And friendſhip's altar ever blaze.

Begone, begone, fly diſcord hence,
With party rage and inſolence :
Sweet peace ſhall bleſs this happy band,
And freedom ſmile throughout the land.

SONG III.
[*Tune*, Rule Britannia.]

WHEN earth's foundation firſt was laid,
  By the almighty Artiſt's hand,
'Twas then our perfect, our perfect laws were made,
  Eſtabliſhed by his ſtrict command.
Chor. Hail, myſterious ; hail, glorious Maſonry !
    That makes us ever great and free.

As man throughout for ſhelter ſought,
  In vain from place to place did roam,
Until from heaven, from heaven he was taught
  To plan, to build, to fix his home.
              Hail, myſterious, &c.

Hence illuſtrious roſe our Art,
  And now in beauteous piles appear ;
Which ſhall to endleſs, to endleſs time impart,
  How worthy and how great we are.
              Hail, myſterious, &c.

Nor we less fam'd for every tye,
  By which the human thought is bound;
Love, truth, and friendship, and friendship socially,
  Join all our hearts and hands around.
Hail, mysterious, &c.

Our actions still by virtue blest,
  And to our precepts ever true,
The world admiring, admiring shall request
  To learn, and our bright paths pursue.
Hail, mysterious, &c.

SONG IV.

[*Tune*, Goddess of Ease.]

GENIUS of Masonry descend,
  And with thee bring thy spotless train;
Constant our sacred rites attend,
  While we adore thy peaceful reign:
Bring with thee Virtue, brightest maid,
  Bring Love, bring Truth, and Friendship here;
While social Mirth shall lend her aid,
  To smooth the wrinkled brow of Care.

Come, Charity, with goodness crown'd,
  Encircled in thy heav'nly robe,
Diffuse thy blessings all around,
  To ev'ry corner of the globe:
See where she comes, with power to bless,
  With open hand and tender heart,
Which wounded is at man's distress,
  And bleeds at ev'ry human smart.

Envy may ev'ry ill devife,
  And Falfhood be thy deadlieft foe,
Thou Friendfhip ftill fhalt tow'ring rife,
  And fink thine adverfaries low;
Thy well-built pile fhall long endure,
  Through rolling years preferve its prime,
Upon a rock it ftands fecure,
  And braves the rude affaults of Time.

Ye happy few, who here extend
  In perfect lines from eaft to weft,
With fervent zeal the lodge defend,
  And lock its fecrets in each breaft:
Since ye are met upon the fquare,
  Bid love and friendfhip jointly reign,
Be peace and harmony your care,
  Nor break the adamantine chain.

Behold the planets how they move,
  Yet keep due order as they run;
Then imitate the ftars above,
  And fhine refplendent as the fun:
That future Mafons when they meet,
  May all our glorious deeds rehearfe,
And fay, their fathers were fo great,
  That they adorn'd the univerfe.

SONG V.

ON, on, my dear brethren, purfue your great lecture,
And refine on the rules of old architecture;
High honour to Mafons the Craft daily brings,
To thofe brothers of Princes and fellows of Kings.

We

We drove the rude Vandals and Goths off the stage,
Reviving the Art of Augustus' fam'd age;
And Vespasian destroy'd the vast temple in vain,
Since so many now rise in Lord Petre's mild reign.

The noble five orders, compos'd with such art,
Will amaze the fix'd eye, and engage the whole heart;
Proportion's sweet harmony gracing the whole,
Gives our work, like the glorious creation, a soul.

Then Master and brethren preserve your great name,
This Lodge so majestic will purchase you fame;
Rever'd it shall stand till all nature expire,
And its glories ne'er fade till the world is on fire.

See, see, behold here, what rewards all our toil,
Inspires our genius, and bids labour smile:
To our noble Grand Master we're solemnly bound,
With honour we're deck'd, and with virtue we're crown'd.

Again, my lov'd brethren, again, let it pass,
Our ancient firm union cements with the glass:
And all the contention 'mongst Masons shall be,
Who better can work, or who better agree.

SONG VI.

HAIL Masonry, thou Craft divine!
   Glory of earth, from heav'n reveal'd;
Which doth with jewels precious shine,
   From all but Masons' eyes conceal'd:
     Thy praises due, who can rehearse,
     In nervous prose, or flowing verse?

All Craftsmen true, distinguish'd are,
  Our laws all other laws excel;
And what's in knowledge choice and rare,
  Within our breasts securely dwell.
    The silent breast, the faithful heart,
    Preserve the secrets of the Art.

From scorching heat and piercing cold,
  From beasts, whose roar the forest rends;
From the assault of warriors bold,
  The Masons' Art mankind defends.
    Be to this Art due honour paid,
    From which mankind receives such aid.

Ensigns of state that feed our pride,
  Distinctions troublesome and vain,
By Masons true are laid aside,
  Art's free born sons such toys disdain.
    Ennobled by the name they bear,
    Distinguish'd by the *badge* they wear.

Sweet fellowship, from envy free,
  Friendly converse of brotherhood;
The lodge's lasting cement be,
  Which has for ages firmly stood.
    A lodge thus built, for ages past
    Has lasted, and shall ever last.

Then in our songs be justice done
  To those who have enrich'd the Art,
From Adam to Lord Petre down,
  And let each brother bear a part.
    Let noble Masons' healths go round,
    Their praise in lofty lodge resound.

Chor.

Chor. No Craft with Masons can compare,
 Ennobled by the *badge* they wear.
No Craft with Masons can compare,
 Distinguish'd by the *badge* they wear.
No Craft with Masons can compare,
 Let none despise the *badge* they wear.

SONG VII.

[*Tune*, In Infancy, &c.]

LET Masonry from pole to pole
 Her sacred laws expand,
Far as the mighty waters roll,
 To wash remotest land:
That virtue has not left mankind,
 Her social maxims prove,
For stamp'd upon the Mason's mind,
 Are Unity and Love.

Ascending to her native sky,
 Let Masonry increase;
A glorious pillar rais'd on high,
 Integrity its base.
Peace adds to olive boughs, entwin'd,
 An emblematic dove,
As stamp'd upon the Masons' mind
 Are Unity and Love.

SONG VIII.

'TIS Masonry unites mankind,
 To generous actions forms the soul;
So strict in union we're conjoin'd,
 One spirit animates the whole.

Chor.

Chor. Then let mankind our deeds approve,
   Since union, harmony, and love
   Shall waft us to the realms above.

Where'er aspiring domes arise,
   Wherever sacred altars stand,
Those altars blaze up to the skies,
   Those domes proclaim the mason's hand.

The stone unshap'd as lumber lies,
   Till masons' art its form refines;
So passions do our souls disguise,
   Till social virtue calms our minds.

Let wretches at our manhood rail;
   But those who once our judgment prove,
Will own that we who build so well,
   With equal energy can love.

Though still our chief concern and care,
   Be to deserve a brother's name;
For ever mindful of the fair,
   Their choicest favours still we claim.

From us pale Discord long has fled,
   With all her train of mortal spite;
Nor in our lodge dares shew her head,
   Sunk in the gloom of endless night.

My brethren charge your glasses high,
   To our Grand Master's noble name;
Our shouts shall beat the vaulted sky,
   And ev'ry tongue his praise proclaim.

SONG.

SONG IX.

[*Tune*, God save the King.]

LET Masons' fame resound
Thro' all the nations round,
    From pole to pole:
See what felicity,
Harmless simplicity,
Like electricity,
    Runs thro' the whole.

Such sweet variety
Ne'er had society
    Ever before:
Faith, hope, and charity,
Love and sincerity,
Without temerity,
    Charm more and more.

When in the lodge we're met,
And in due order set,
    Happy are we:
Our works are glorious,
Deeds meritorious,
Never censorious,
    But great and free.

When Folly's sons arise,
Masonry to despise,
    Scorn all their spite;
Laugh at their ignorance,
Pity their want of sense,
Ne'er let them give offence,
    Firmer unite.

Masons have long been free,
And may they ever be
   Great as of yore:
For many ages past,
Masonry has stood fast,
And may its glory last,
   Till time's no more.

SONG X.

[*Tune*, God save the King.]

HAIL, Masonry divine;
Glory of ages shine,
   Long may'st thou reign:
Where'er thy Lodges stand,
May they have great command,
And always grace the land,
   Thou Art divine!

Great fabrics still arise,
And grace the azure skies,
   Great are thy schemes:
Thy noble orders are
Matchless beyond compare;
No Art with thee can share,
   Thou Art divine!

Hiram, the architect,
Did all the Craft direct
   How they should build;
Sol'mon, great Isr'el's king,
Did mighty blessings bring, } *Chorus* 3 *times.*
And left us room to sing,
   Hail, royal Art!

SONG XI.

LET drunkards boast the pow'r of wine,
   And reel from side to side;
Let lovers kneel at Beauty's shrine,
   The sport of female pride:
Be ours the more exalted part,
To celebrate the Masons' Art,
   And spread its praises wide.

To dens and thickets dark and rude,
   For shelter beasts repair;
With sticks and straws the feather'd brood,
   Suspend their nests in air:
And man untaught, as wild as these,
Binds up sad huts with boughs of trees,
   And feeds on wretched fare.

But Science dawning in his mind,
   The quarry he explores;
Industry and the Arts combin'd,
   Improv'd all Nature's stores:
Thus walls were built, and houses rear'd,
No storms or tempests now are fear'd
   Within his well-fram'd doors.

When stately palaces arise,
   When columns grace the hall,
When tow'rs and spires salute the skies,
   We owe to Masons all:
Nor buildings only do they give,
But teach men how within to live,
   And yield to Reason's call.

All party quarrels they detest,
  For Virtue and the Arts,
Lodg'd in each true Free Mason's breast,
  Unite and rule their hearts:
By these, while Masons square their minds,
The State no better subjects finds,
  None act more upright parts.

When Bucks and Albions are forgot,
  Free-Masons will remain;
Mushrooms, each day, spring up and rot,
  While oaks stretch o'er the plain:
Let others quarrel, rant, and roar;
Their noisy revels when no more,
  Still Masonry shall reign.

Our leathern aprons may compare
  With Garters red or blue;
Princes and Kings our brothers are,
  May they our rules pursue:
Then drink success and health to all
The Craft around this Earthly Ball,
  May Brethren still prove true.

SONG XII.

COME let us prepare,
  We brothers that are
Assembled on merry occasion:
  Let's be happy and sing,
  For Life is a Spring
To a Free and an Accepted Mason.

The world is in pain
Our secrets to gain,
And still let them wonder and gaze on:
They ne'er can divine
The Word or the Sign
Of a Free and an Accepted Mason.

'Tis this and 'tis that,
They cannot tell what,
Nor why the great men of the nation,
Should aprons put *on*,
To make themselves one
With a Free and an Accepted Mason.

Great Kings, Dukes, and Lords,
Have laid by their swords,
Our myst'ry to put a good grace on;
And ne'er been asham'd
To hear themselves nam'd
With a Free and an Accepted Mason.

Antiquity's pride
We have on our side,
To keep up our old reputation;
There's nought but what's good
To be understood
By a Free and an Accepted Mason.

We're true and sincere,
And just to the Fair;
They'll trust us on any occasion:
No mortal can more
The ladies adore,
Than a Free and an Accepted Mason.

Then join hand in hand,
  By each brother firm stand,
Let's be merry and put a bright face on;
  What mortal can boast
  So noble a toast
As a Free and an Accepted Mason.

Chor. No mortal can boast
  So noble a toast
As a Free and an Accepted Mason.

SONG XIII.

TO all who Masonry despise,
  This counsel I bestow;
Don't ridicule, if you are wise,
  A secret you don't know.
Yourselves you banter, and not it;
You shew your spleen, but not your wit.
  With a fa, la, la, la, la, la.

If union and sincerity
  Have a pretence to please,
We brothers of Free-Masonry,
  Lay justly claim to these.
To state disputes we ne'er give birth,
Our motto friendship is, and mirth.

Inspiring virtue by our rules,
  And in ourselves secure,
We have compassion on those fools
  Who think our acts impure:
From ignorance we know proceeds
Such mean opinion of our deeds.

SONG XIV.

YE thrice happy few
  Whose hearts have been true,
In concord and unity found;
  Let us sing and rejoice,
  And unite ev'ry voice,
To send the gay chorus around.

Chorus.

Like pillars we stand,
  An immovable band,
Cemented by pow'r from above;
  Then freely let pass
  The generous glass
To Masonry, Friendship, and Love.

The GRAND ARCHITECT,
  Whose word did erect
Eternity, measure, and space,
  First laid the fair plan
  Whereon we began
The cement of friendship and peace.

Whose firmness of hearts,
  Fair treasure of arts,
To the eye of the vulgar unknown;
  Whose lustre can beam
  New splendor and fame
To the pulpit, the bar, and the throne.

The great David's son,
Unmatch'd Solomon,
As written in Scripture's bright page,
A Mason became,
The fav'rite of Fame,
The wonder and pride of his age.

Indissoluble bands,
Our hearts and our hands
In social benevolence bind;
For true to his cause,
By immutable laws,
A Mason's a friend to mankind.

Let Joy flow around,
And Peace, olive-bound,
Preside at our mystical rites,
Whose conduct maintains
Our auspicious domains,
And Freedom with Order unites.

Nor let the dear maid
Our mysteries dread,
Or think them repugnant to love;
To Beauty we bend,
Her empire defend,
An empire deriv'd from above.

Then let us unite,
Sincere and upright,
On the level of virtue to stand:
No mortal can be
So happy as we
With a brother and friend in each hand.

SONG

SONG XV.

WHEN a lodge of Free-Masons are cloath'd in their aprons,
   In order to make a new brother,
With firm hearts and clean hands they repair to their stands,
   And justly support one another.

Trusty Brother take care, of eve-droppers beware,
   Tis a just and a solemn occasion;
Give the Word and the Blow, that workmen may know,
   There's one asks to be made a Free-Mason.

The Master stands due, and his officers too,
   While the craftsmen are plying their station;
The apprentices stand right for the command
   Of a Free and an Accepted Mason.

Now traverse your ground, as in duty you're bound,
   And revere the authentic oration,
That leads to the way, and proves the first ray
   Of the light of an Accepted Mason.

Here's Words, and here's Signs, and here's Problems
   and Lines,
   And here's room too for deep speculation;
Here Virtue and Truth are taught to the Youth,
   When first he's call'd up to a Mason.

Hieroglyphics shine bright, and here light reverts
   On the Rules and the Tools of vocation; [light,
We work and we sing the Craft and the King,
   'Tis both duty and choice in a Mason.

What is said or is done, is here truly laid down,
    In this form of our high installation;
Yet I challenge all men to know what I mean,
    Unless he's an Accepted Mason.

The Ladies claim right to come into our light,
    Since the Apron, they say, is their bearing;
Can they subject their will? can they keep their
        tongues still?
    And let talking be chang'd into hearing?

This difficult task is the least we can ask,
    To secure us on sundry occasions;
When with this they comply, our utmost we'll try
    To raise lodges for Lady Free Masons.

Till this can be done, must each brother be mum,
    Though the fair one should wheedle or teaze on;
Be just, true, and kind, but still bear in mind,
    At all times that you are a **Free-Mason**.

SONG XVI.

HOW happy a Mason whose bosom still flows
With friendship, and ever most cheerfully goes,
Th' effects of the mysteries lodg'd in his breast,
Mysteries rever'd, and by Princes possest.
Our friends and our bottle we best can enjoy,
No rancour or envy our quiet annoy,
Our plumb-line and compass, our square and our
    tools,
Direct all our actions in Virtue's fair rules,
Direct all our actions, &c.

To Mars and to Venus we're equally true,
Our hearts can enliven, our arms can subdue,
Let the enemy tell, and the ladies declare,
No clafs or profeffion with Mafons compare;
To give a fond luftre we ne'er need a creft,
Since Honour and Virtue remain in our breaft,
We'll charm the rude world when we clap, laugh,
    and fing,
If fo happy a Mafon, fay who'd be a King.
If fo happy, &c.

SONG XVII.

[*Tune*, Balance a Straw.]

WHEN the Sun from the eaft firft falutes mortal eyes,
And the fky-lark melodioufly bids us arife;
With our hearts full of joy, we the fummons obey,
Straight repair to our work, and to moiften our clay.

On the traffel our Mafter draws angles and lines,
There with freedom and fervency forms his defigns;
Not a picture on earth is fo lovely to view,
All his lines are fo perfect, his angles fo true.

In the weft, fee the Wardens fubmiffively ftand,
The Mafter to aid, and obey his command;
The intent of his fignals we perfectly know,
And we ne'er take offence when he gives us a blow.

In the lodge, sloth and dulness we always avoid,
Fellow-crafts and apprentices all are employ'd:
Perfect ashlers some finish, some make the rough plain,
All are pleas'd with their work, and are pleas'd with their gain.

When my Master I've serv'd seven years, perhaps more,
Some secrets he'll tell me I ne'er knew before;
In my bosom I'll keep them as long as I live,
And pursue the directions his wisdom shall give.

I'll attend to his call both by night and by day,
It is his to command, and 'tis mine to obey;
Whensoe'er we are met, I'll attend to his nod,
And I'll work till high twelve, then I'll lay down my hod.

THE END.

Bibliography

Prepared by WALTER M. CALLAWAY, JR.

Preston, William—*Illustrations of Masonry*, 1775

Webb, Thomas Smith—*Illustrations of Masonry or Freemasons Monitor*, 1802

Georgia—*Masonic Manual and Code*, 1963

Grand Lodge, *1717-1967, U.G.L. of England*

The Collected Prestonian Lectures, 1925-1960

Coil, Henry W.—*Masonic Encyclopedia*, 1961

Mackey, Albert—*Encyclopedia of Freemasonry*, 1874

Cross, Jeremy—*The True Masonic Chart or Hieroglyphic Monitor*, 1850 ed.

Leyland, Herbert T.—*Thomas Smith Webb*, 1963

Hills, G. P. G.—*Bro. Wm. Preston: An Illustration of the Man and His Methods and His Work*, 41 AQC 163-184 (1928)

Horne, Alex—*William Preston's Lectures on the Five Orders of Architecture: Its Origin and Development*, 77 AQC 105-143 (1964)

James, P. R.—*The Lectures of English Craft Freemasonry*, 79 AQC 140-179 (1966)

Pick, P. L.—*Preston—The Gild and the Craft*, 59 AQC 90-126 (1946)

Saul, J. B.—*Preston's Illustrations of Masonry*, 24 AQC 71-72 (1911)

Worts, F. R.—*Preston's Advertisement of his Private Lectures on Masonry in Twelve Courses*, 73 AQC 115-116 (1960)

Worts, F. R.—*Preston's Use of Leslie's Work*, 73 AQC 120-123 (1960)

Gale, Jas. B.—*Wm. Preston, Masonic Historian, Ritualist and Patron; A Paper for Mystic Tie Academy*, Indianapolis, Ind., 1971

COLOPHON

Five hundred and fifty-five copies of this limited edition were manufactured by the Pantagraph Press and Bloomington Offset Process, Inc., both of Bloomington, Illinois. The former did the composition and binding and the latter the facsimile plates and the presswork.

The type faces used for the type-set portion of this book are of the Linotype Janson and Monotype Caslon families.

The text paper used is sixty pound basis white wove Warren's Olde Style manufactured by the S. D. Warren Company. The book covers are made of Columbia Mills' Riverside Vellum over boards and stamped in genuine gold.

All volumes of The Masonic Book Club series were designed and prepared by Louis L. Williams, Alphonse Cerza, and Fred A. Dolan.

Related Titles from Westphalia Press

Ancient Mysteries and Modern Masonry: The Collected Writings of Jewel P. Lightfoot, Edited by Billy J. Hamilton Jr.

Jewel P. Lightfoot. Former Attorney General of the State of Texas. Past Grand Master of the Masonic Grand Lodge of Texas. From humble beginnings in rural Arkansas, he worked to become an educated man who excelled in law and Freemasonry. He was a gentleman of his time, well-known as a scholar, public speaker, and Masonic philosopher.

Essay on The Mysteries and the True Object of The Brotherhood of Freemasons
by Jason Williams

This isn't a reprint of a classic. It's a new rendition with new life breathed into it, to be enjoyed both by the layperson trying to understand the Craft and Masonic scholars taking a deeper dive into the fraternity's golden years—when the concepts of liberty and equality were still fresh.

Female Emancipation and Masonic Membership:
An Essential Collection
By Guillermo De Los Reyes Heredia

Female Emancipation and Masonic Membership: An Essential Combination is a collection of essays on Freemasonry and gender that promotes a transatlantic discussion of the study of the history of women and Freemasonry and their contribution in different countries.

Freemasonry, Heir to the Enlightenment
by Cécile Révauger

Modern Freemasonry may have mythical roots in Solomon's time but is really the heir to the Enlightenment. Ever since the early eighteenth century freemasons have endeavored to convey the values of the Enlightenment in the cultural, political and religious fields, in Europe, the American colonies and the emerging United States.

Freemasonry: A French View
by Roger Dachez and Alain Bauer

Perhaps one should speak not of Freemasonry but of Freemasonries in the plural. In each country Masonic historiography has developed uniqueness. Two of the best known French Masonic scholars present their own view of the worldwide evolution and challenging mysteries of the fraternity over the centuries.

Worlds of Print: The Moral Imagination of an Informed Citizenry, 1734 to 1839
by John Slifko

John Slifko argues that freemasonry was representative and played an important role in a larger cultural transformation of literacy and helped articulate the moral imagination of an informed democratic citizenry via fast emerging worlds of print.

Why Thirty-Three?: Searching for Masonic Origins
by S. Brent Morris, PhD

What "high degrees" were in the United States before 1830? What were the activities of the Order of the Royal Secret, the precursor of the Scottish Rite? A complex organization with a lengthy pedigree like Freemasonry has many basic foundational questions waiting to be answered, and that's what this book does: answers questions.

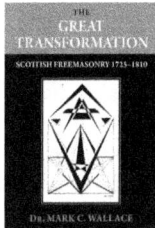
The Great Transformation: Scottish Freemasonry 1725-1810
by Dr. Mark C. Wallace

This book examines Scottish Freemasonry in its wider British and European contexts between the years 1725 and 1810. The Enlightenment effectively crafted the modern mason and propelled Freemasonry into a new era marked by growing membership and the creation of the Grand Lodge of Scotland.

Getting the Third Degree: Fraternalism, Freemasonry and History
Edited by Guillermo De Los Reyes and Paul Rich

As this engaging collection demonstrates, the doors being opened on the subject range from art history to political science to anthropology, as well as gender studies, sociology and more. The organizations discussed may insist on secrecy, but the research into them belies that.

A Place in the Lodge: Dr. Rob Morris, Freemasonry and the Order of the Eastern Star
by Nancy Stearns Theiss, PhD

Ridiculed as "petticoat masonry," critics of the Order of the Eastern Star did not deter Rob Morris' goal to establish a Masonic organization that included women as members. Morris carried the ideals of Freemasonry through a despairing time of American history.

Brought to Light: The Mysterious George Washington Masonic Cave
by Jason Williams MD

The George Washington Masonic Cave near Charles Town, West Virginia, contains a signature carving of George Washington dated 1748. This book painstakingly pieces together the chronicled events and real estate archives related to the cavern in order to sort out fact from fiction.

Dudley Wright: Writer, Truthseeker & Freemason
by John Belton

Dudley Wright (1868-1950) was an Englishman and professional journalist who took a universalist approach to the various great Truths of Life. He travelled though many religions in his life and wrote about them all, but was probably most at home with Islam.

History of the Grand Orient of Italy
Emanuela Locci, Editor

No book in Masonic literature upon the history of Italian Freemasonry has been edited in English up to now. This work consists of eight studies, covering a span from the Eighteenth Century to the end of the WWII, tracing through the story, the events and pursuits related to the Grand Orient of Italy.

westphaliapress.org

Policy Studies Organization

The Policy Studies Organization (PSO) is a publisher of academic journals and book series, sponsor of conferences, and producer of programs.

Policy Studies Organization publishes dozens of journals on a range of topics, such as European Policy Analysis, Journal of Elder Studies, Indian Politics & Polity, Journal of Critical Infrastructure Policy, and Popular Culture Review.

Additionally, Policy Studies Organization hosts numerous conferences. These conferences include the Middle East Dialogue, Space Education and Strategic Applications Conference, International Criminology Conference, Dupont Summit on Science, Technology and Environmental Policy, World Conference on Fraternalism, Freemasonry and History, and the Internet Policy & Politics Conference.

For more information on these projects, access videos of past events, and upcoming events, please visit us at:

www.ipsonet.org

www.ingramcontent.com/pod-product-compliance
Lightning Source LLC
Chambersburg PA
CBHW051525020426
42333CB00016B/1777